Improving Group Decision Making in Organizations

APPROACHES FROM THEORY AND RESEARCH

ORGANIZATIONAL AND OCCUPATIONAL PSYCHOLOGY

Series Editor: PETER WARR
MRC Social and Applied Psychology Unit, Department of Psychology,
The University, Sheffield, England

Theodore D. Weinshall
Managerial Communication: Concepts, Approaches and Techniques, 1979

Chris Argyris
Inner Contradictions of Rigorous Research, 1980

Charles J. de Wolff, Sylvia Shimmin, and Maurice de Montmollin
Conflicts and Contradictions: Work Psychology in Europe, 1981

Nigel Nicholson, Gil Ursell, and Paul Blyton
The Dynamics of White Collar Unionism, 1981

Dean G. Pruitt
Negotiation Behavior, 1981

Richard T. Mowday, Lyman W. Porter, and Richard M. Steers
Employee–Organization Linkages: The Psychology of Commitment,
Absenteeism, and Turnover, 1982

Richard A. Guzzo (Editor)
Improving Group Decision Making in Organizations: Approaches from
Theory and Research, 1982

In preparation

George C. Thornton III and William C. Byham
Assessment Centers and Managerial Performance, 1982

Improving Group Decision Making in Organizations

APPROACHES FROM THEORY AND RESEARCH

Edited by

RICHARD A. GUZZO

Department of Psychology
New York University
New York, New York

 1982

ACADEMIC PRESS
A Subsidiary of Harcourt Brace Jovanovich, Publishers
New York   London
Paris San Diego San Francisco São Paulo Sydney Tokyo Toronto

77401

ACADEMIC PRESS, INC.
111 Fifth Avenue, New York, New York 10003

United Kingdom Edition published by
ACADEMIC PRESS, INC. (LONDON) LTD.
24/28 Oval Road, London NW1 7DX

Library of Congress Cataloging in Publication Data
Main entry under title:

Improving group decision making in organizations.

   (Organizational and occupational psychology)
   Includes bibliographies and index.
   1. Decision-making, Group. I. Guzzo, Richard A.
II. Series.
HD30.23.I4   658.4'036   81-22827
ISBN 0-12-310980-9   AACR2

Contents

3

Group Remembering: Research and Implications

JON HARTWICK, BLAIR H. SHEPPARD, and JAMES H. DAVIS

4

Game Theory and the Structure of Decision-Making Groups

J. KEITH MURNIGHAN

5

Improving the Problem-Solving Process in Managerial Groups

L. RICHARD HOFFMAN

6

Creativity, Groups, and Management

MORRIS I. STEIN

List of Contributors

Numbers in parentheses indicate the pages on which the authors' contributions begin.

RICHARD L. COOK (13), Institute of Behavioral Science, Center for Research on Judgment and Policy, University of Colorado, Boulder, Colorado 80309

JAMES H. DAVIS (41), Department of Psychology, University of Illinois at Urbana–Champaign, Champaign, Illinois 61820

RICHARD A. GUZZO (1), Department of Psychology, New York University, New York, New York 10003

KENNETH R. HAMMOND (13), Institute of Behavioral Science, Center for Research on Judgment and Policy, University of Colorado, Boulder, Colorado 80309

JON HARTWICK (41), Faculty of Management, McGill University, Montreal, PQ, Canada H3A 1G5

L. RICHARD HOFFMAN (95), Graduate School of Management, Rutgers University, Newark, New Jersey 07102

J. KEITH MURNIGHAN (73), Department of Business Administration, University of Illinois at Urbana–Champaign, Champaign, Illinois 61820

BLAIR H. SHEPPARD[1] (41), Faculty of Management, McGill University, Montreal, PQ, Canada H3A 1G5

MORRIS I. STEIN (127), Department of Psychology, New York University, New York, New York 10003

---

[1] *Present address:* Fuqua School of Business, Duke University, Durham, North Carolina 27514.

Preface

Group decision making is not a simple matter. It is a product of the cognitive processing of information, norms influencing the nature of social interaction, the skills, traits, and dispositions of individual group members, and more. And like the proverbial blind men describing the elephant, researchers attending to different aspects of group decision making produce seemingly disparate portraits of the overall process. Alone, these portraits suggest competing, incompatible views of the group decision process. Together, their complementary relationship becomes apparent, as does the fruitfulness of examining group decision making from a variety of perspectives.

This book brings together advances in our understanding of decision-making groups, especially those found in organizations, and identifies ways of making such groups more effective. The first chapter reviews the history of the study of group decision making, some origins of the diversity of approaches adopted in its study, and the nature of interventions to improve it. The second through sixth chapters concern different parts of the whole, such as the processing of information, the dynamics of selecting among alternatives, the role of power differences in decision-making groups, and creativity. Each chapter addresses the current state of knowledge in a particular area and the practical implications of that work for aiding decision-making groups.

The book's audience, then, is a broad one. It is of interest to those students and active researchers who seek to understand further the psychology of group decision making. It is also of interest to those who manage decision-making groups in organizational settings and to those who make use of interventions to improve group performance. There is no rift between research and practice in this volume.

This book is an outgrowth, but not a proceedings, of a symposium on group decision making sponsored by the Faculty of Management of McGill University while the editor was a member of that faculty. I wish to acknowledge the generous support of that institution, especially the support of my friend, Rabi Kanungo, whose encouragement made possible the symposium and the book.

1

The Study of Group Decision Making: Approaches and Applications

RICHARD A. GUZZO

The study of group decision making is both fascinating and important. It is fascinating because the action of decision-making groups can be puzzling and unpredictable; it is important because this action often has significant consequences. Group decision making in government and industry, for example, can influence our lives in many ways, such as through the establishment of laws and rules and the determination of how much we are paid for our work. This book is about ways of understanding the tangle of activities in group decision making and using this knowledge to improve decision making, and thus improve our lives.

Many people and perspectives appear in the study of group decision making, leading to diverse tactics for improving it. In this chapter, I examine the history of the study of group decision making to identify sources of this diversity of approaches and to describe differences among them. Also, the nature of attempts to improve the performance of decision-making groups is discussed, and consideration is given to the role of theory in the formulation of strategies for improving group decision making. Finally, the subsequent chapters of the book are introduced in the context of this chapter's concerns.

IMPROVING GROUP DECISION MAKING IN ORGANIZATIONS

An Historical View of the Study of Group
Decision Making

THE TIE TO GROUP DYNAMICS

The history of the systematic study of group decision making aligns closely with the history of the study of group dynamics in general. Group dynamics, as defined by Cartwright and Zander (1968), is a field of inquiry that seeks to advance knowledge about the nature of groups and especially about the psychological and social forces associated with them. It is a field broadly bounded, populated by individuals of divergent backgrounds and pursuits, in which decision making is only one of many concerns. Though diverse, the field coheres because its members share an emphasis on theoretically significant research, a view of group behavior as consisting of interdependent and dynamic elements, an appreciation of the merit of an interdisciplinary approach to the study of groups, and a special attention given to the applicability of research findings and theory for social practice (Cartwright & Zander, 1968). These characteristics describe well the nature of the study of group decision making.

Without much warning, as Zander (1979a) puts it, a powerful interest in how groups behave developed in the 1930s and surged through the 1940s and 1950s. This was evidenced by an ever-increasing annual rate of publications about groups during these decades. However, research interest in groups declined during the 1960s and 1970s, with the number of publications per year falling below the level found in the 1950s. Indicative of this is the title of a recent special volume of the *Journal of Applied Behavioral Science:* "What's Happened to Small Group Research?" (Volume 15, Number 3, 1979).

Group decision making was not frequently studied during the first three decades of group dynamics research, even though antecedents of today's interest in it appear in studies reported during these years contrasting individual and group abilities to solve problems and make judgments (e.g., Gordon, 1924; Knight, 1921; Shaw, 1932). These early studies might have provided a springboard for considerable decision-making research during the boom years of the group dynamics field; instead, they yielded to other topics that captured the attention of group dynamics researchers, especially those of leadership, attitude change, interpersonal influence, and pressures for conformity. Decision making, problem solving, and judgment in groups did not emerge as dominant topics of inquiry until recently.

Zander (1979b) notes the appearance of fashions in group dynamics research. Topics receive attention for a while, followed by a remission of interest, only to gain attention once again at a later date. While the topic of group decision making has not experienced exactly such periodicity of interest, it is now a popular target of inquiry. And with good reason. From the point of view of a researcher and theorist, it is a topic well tailored for the group dynamics investigatory approach. Its complexity calls for the development of theory, it is composed of numerous dynamic, interdependent elements, and it is fruitfully examined from an interdisciplinary orientation. From a practitioner's point of view, the application of research findings for the improvement of group decision making is of great importance. In light of this, one is left to wonder why it took so long for group decision making to fire the interest of group dynamics researchers.

THE DIVERSITY OF APPROACHES

As earlier mentioned, a variety of views are adopted in the study of group dynamics, and Cartwright and Zander (1968) offer reasons why this is so. One is that group research is conducted in many social settings: classrooms, the military, business organizations, therapy groups, and so on. Consequently, "it is only to be expected that different investigators will emphasize in their theorizing different phenomena and explanatory principles [p. 28]." Another reason is that different social problems prompt different emphases in theorists. Examining intergroup conflict, for example, leads investigators to a different theoretical orientation than does examining productivity in work groups. A third reason why such diversity of perspectives persists is that when many disciplines mingle, as in the study of groups, members of the various disciplines bring with them different vocabularies and assumptions about groups, which are difficult to reconcile. While providing energy and interest to the field, these differences may also preclude any full integration of theoretical approaches to group dynamics.

The same sources of diversity in the general group dynamics field also bring about highly varied perspectives in the study of decision making. For example, the range of social settings in which group decision making is investigated—political bodies, juries, business organizations—leads to different emphases in its study, as do differences in vocabularies and assumptions among the theoretical orientations of researchers (e.g., those of game theoretic and interpersonal competence theoretic orientations). Also, the complexity of the decision-making phenomenon itself sustains the diversity of perspectives found in the study of decision making. Some researchers focus on the process by which alternative solutions are generated by a group, some on the selection among alternatives, some on the role of the leader in a group, some on the stressfulness of decision making. This array of topics indicates just how multifaceted the group decision-making process is and how many things there are to learn about it.

THE COMMONALITY OF APPROACHES

Regardless of the particular theoretical orientation adopted in the study of group decision making, investigators share the task of addressing two major issues. One is the processing of information. When we speak of decision making, whether with reference to individuals, groups, organizations, governments, or any other entity, of necessity we speak of information processing. This includes collecting and evaluating information, forging alternative courses of action, and selecting one as preferred. The study of groups as decision makers, however, entails a second focus: the social–psychological dynamics of behavior. All attempts to understand group decision making must address both issues.

There is a strong mutuality of influence between information-handling activities and social psychological forces. How information is acquired and evaluated can limit the nature of the social interaction among group members. For example, a procedure for reaching planning decisions in groups called the Nominal Group Technique (NGT, Delbecq, Van den Ven, & Gustafson, 1975) imposes strict guidelines concerning how information is to be managed and these guidelines in turn limit the ways in which social influence can take place among group members. Conversely, the impact of social–psychological forces on information processing is illustrated in the work of Janis (1972). Janis identifies a syndrome called "groupthink," in which flawed information processing results from social–psychological forces for concurrence seeking among group members. Janis also discusses the positive impact of within-group forces on the handling of information. Different perspectives on group decision making, then, ultimately address the interrelationship of information-processing activities and the dynamics of behavior in small groups in order to be able to understand and improve group decision making, although theories differ in the adoption of either of those two elements as the starting point in their analysis.

SUMMARY

It can be seen, then, that the study of group decision making has strong ties to the history of the field of group dynamics. Some of the factors inducing a wide range of theoretical orientations to appear in the group dynamics field also induce varied theoretical orientations in the study of group decision making; the complex nature of the group decision-making phenomenon itself also fosters this diversity of orientations. The approaches in the study of group decision making, however, have the common task of addressing the interaction of social behavior and information processing.

The various theoretical orientations also have led to a wide array of prescriptions, interventions, and techniques designed to increase the performance effectiveness of decision-making groups. Discussed next is the nature of efforts to apply theory and research findings for the improvement of group decision making.

Some Applications of Theory and Research

While an important mark of the progress of the study of group decision making is its social utility, it is necessary to recognize that, on the whole, investigation into the social utility of theory and research on the topic is nascent. Relatively few studies exist, and most of these have been conducted under controlled laboratory conditions rather than in business and government organizations, juries, and other natural settings in which utility ultimately is tested. As Hoffman (1979) suggests, extrapolating the results of current research to group decision making in organizational settings may be "fraught with danger and the conclusions should be accepted with utmost caution [p. 386]." Still, it is instructive to examine this research while cognizant of its limitations.

TWO TYPES OF INTERVENTIONS

Interventions to improve group decision making can be regarded as being of two types on the basis of their primary target: the action of, or inputs to, group decision making. The first type has as its target direct changes in the behavior of decision-making group members. These changes could be brought about by the creation of new patterns of social interaction, or by the establishment of specific procedures of task accomplishment, for example, requiring groups to adhere to a sequence of steps such as defining the problem, generating alternatives, and then evaluating and choosing among alternatives. Thus, such interventions can affect either or both the social–psychological influences residing in a group and the processes of manipulating and utilizing information.

Input-oriented interventions, the second type, also seek to change behavior in groups, but they attempt to do this indirectly rather than directly. Inputs to group decision include the distribution of abilities and vested interests among group members, the nature of available information, group size, the reward structure under which a group exists, and time pressures for decision making. Thus it is possible to intervene to arrange inputs and circumstances such that effective decision making will be more likely, without explicitly specifying new patterns of behavior for group members. As with action-oriented interventions, the consequences of input-oriented interventions can affect information processing and social–psychological factors in a group.

It is important to recognize that these two types of interventions can be, and often are, made simultaneously. The distinction between the two types is a useful heuristic for examining the utility of efforts to improve group decision making, not a statement of independence of the two.

EXAMPLES OF ACTION-ORIENTED INTERVENTIONS

Hall and Watson (1970) state that "few articles have appeared in the literature which deal with the modication of group decision making processes [p. 299]" in the interest of more effective functioning. The study reported by Hall and Watson, however, is a good early example of such work. They demonstrated that the performance of decision-making groups that received special instructions designed to alter the interpersonal behavior of group members was superior to that of uninstructed groups. These instructions established new behaviors for handling conflict in groups and the manner of presenting individuals' points of view. As Eils and John (1980) point out, the intervention of this study essentially concerned the communication process in groups and produced considerable increments in performance.

A second example of an action-oriented intervention to improve group decisions is the forced separation of idea generation from idea evaluation. Maier (1963, 1970) was an early proponent of the utility of this separation, and a number of research projects support his view (for reviews see Delbecq *et al.*, 1975; Maier, 1970; Vroom, Grant, & Cotton, 1969). Separating idea generation from evaluation is beneficial to group decision making because it forces a group to examine extensively the nature of the problem, promotes the appearance of many possible solutions for a group's consideration, and decreases the tendency of groups to be "solution-minded," that is, to rush toward the adoption of a solution. This intervention does not concern interpersonal behavior, as did the Hall and Williams (1970) intervention, but rather the sequencing and explicitness of certain information-processing steps necessary for decision making.

The NGT (Delbecq *et al.*, 1975) mentioned earlier also is an action-oriented intervention for improving group decision making. It derives its name from the fact that it severely restricts the amount of free, face-to-face interaction that we typically think of when referring to a group. Thus, to some degree, individuals adopting this technique are a group in name only. In brief, this intervention consists of a sequence of four activities: (a) silent generation of written ideas by group members; (b) recording of ideas in a form visible to all (no discussion here); (c) discussion of each recorded idea for clarification and evaluation; (d) voting on ideas. The group decision is mathematically determined by the results of the voting process. Clearly, this intervention is one of wide scope, and evidence of its effectiveness is reviewed by Delbecq *et al.* (1975).

Some action-oriented interventions are technically sophisticated, especially those with ties to behavioral decision theory (Slovic, Fischoff, & Lichtenstein, 1977). Eils and John (1980), for example, report a study showing that use of the group decision aid of multiattribute utility analysis (MAUA) enhanced the performance of decision-making groups. This procedure requires groups to list alternative courses of action, specify attributes or consequences of the various alternatives, numerically assess the value of each alternative with respect to each attribute, order the attributes in terms of importance, and mathematically combine this information to yield a group decision. It is apparent that the NGT and MAUA interventions strongly shape the form and nature of information used in group decision making, as well as the overt behavior of group members.

EXAMPLES OF INPUT-ORIENTED INTERVENTIONS

An example of this type of intervention is the attempt to enhance the general behavioral and social skills of individuals who find themselves in decision-making groups. In other words, the attempt is to increase the personal resources that an individual carries into a group setting. Research by Hall and Williams (1970) and Schmuck, Runkel, and Langmeyer (1969) provide evidence for the effectiveness of this approach. Schmuck et al. (1969) and Hall and Williams (1970) investigated the effects of laboratory training in group dynamics on the performance of decision-making groups. While the interpersonal skills developed by such training are potentially beneficial to effectiveness in many social situations, not just group decision making, the studies found that such training was in fact related to increased performance in decision-making groups.

Input-oriented interventions can also use sophisticated technology for the processing of information. The work described by Hammond, Rohrbaugh, Mumpower, and Adelman (1977) concerning the application of the principles of Social Judgment Theory (SJT) to aid groups of decision makers in an example of this. The application of SJT involves the quantitative analysis of individuals' preferences among alternative courses of action and goals. Special attention is given to the degree of importance attached to goals, the way in which goals are integrated, and the consistency of individuals' preferences and judgments. Quantitative feedback is provided to decision makers about these factors, as measured for themselves and others in their group. This can be done pictorially through computer-based analyses. In groups, this intervention puts information that was already potentially available to all in a new, organized format, enabling group members to pinpoint areas of agreement and disagreement and thus facilitating the movement toward a decision.

Theory, Research, and Practice

Kurt W. Back (1979), a doyen of group dynamics, suggests that the field of group dynamics now gives too much attention to its applied technology and too little attention to the development of sound theories of groups. According to Back, "the meaning of group dynamics has changed from a science to a profession [p. 284]," in that the field is more concerned with inducing certain effects in groups than with generating basic understandings of them. It is worthwhile to consider whether Back's assertion about the field of group dynamics in general is applicable to the specific area of group decision making.

There is a bond joining research aimed at generating basic knowledge of groups to the application of such findings for the betterment of groups. This bond seems especially strong in the realm of group decision making, for at least three reasons. One, as Cartwright and Zander (1968) point out, is that the field of group dynamics is defined in part by its concurrent emphasis on the building and application of theory. To the extent that the investigation of group decision making is an element of the group dynamics field, there should be compulsion for the generation and application of theories. Second, attempting to change groups helps refine theory when the consequences of those change attempts are monitored. By prescribing interventions and putting them into practice, it is possible to learn what is right or wrong, relevant or irrelevant about the theory underlying the attempted intervention. Working as a "group technologist" helps one's work as a "group theorist" if the consequences of the applications are scrutinized. The third element forming this bond is the strength of the environmentally based force calling for the application of research findings. With regard to group decision making, this force is strong. Making decisions effectively is a prevalent concern, and potential beneficiaries of knowledge about group decision making are eager to see it applied. In contrast, other topics of research in the group dynamics field experience less of a pull for applied knowledge. For example, research results and theories of conformity in groups are not called into action with the same intensity as are those of group decision making. The strength of the pull for applying group decision-making research is not new; its existence was identified over three decades ago by Bradford (1948): "we face problems too big for any of us to meet alone. We stand almost paralyzed before the avalanche of crucial needs for decision and action, which must be made by adults now—and we have not the skills of making these decisions together as they must be made [p. 2]."

Will this pull move theorists and researchers of group decision making into the role of technologists, as Back (1979) suggests has happened in other parts of the group dynamics field? Perhaps, but so far this has not occurred as the subsequent chapters of this book show. There is considerable theoretical advancement taking place in the study of group decision making, and maintaining an awareness of the inherent bond between research and application will ensure a productive future for the study of group decision making.

The Following Chapters and Group Decision Making

In the next chapter, Cook and Hammond view group decision making largely in terms of the processing of information by individual group members. In particular, some of the chief impediments to reaching a decision— conflict, disagreement, and misunderstanding among group members—are regarded as products of the inability of individuals to process information consistently and to understand the positions taken and judgments made by other members about decision issues. This cognitively rooted view stands in contrast to other more social–psychologically oriented views of these impediments to decision making, such as those that interpret conflict as a product of competition among members for dominance. Cook and Hammond suggest a radical input-oriented intervention to aid decision-making groups, one that restructures information for decision making, the goals of which are to explicate each member's thinking and facilitate members' understandings of each other's positions.

In the third chapter, Hartwick, Sheppard, and Davis also give great attention to the information-processing activities of group decision making, as do Cook and Hammond. The focus of the third chapter is on the activities of acquiring, retaining, and recalling information; in short, those of memory. Their concern is with the dynamics of memory from a social–psychological perspective, and they analyze the impact of group membership and behavior on storing and recalling information. They show, for example, that information presented in group settings may be better retained for later use in decision making than that presented to group members separately, and they show that groups biased in their overall memory of information have a lasting, biasing effect on individual memory. Hartwick and his coauthors suggest ways of altering and controlling certain inputs to decision making— recalled information—in the interest of accuracy. These involve managing the social circumstances under which information is put into and recalled from memory.

Murnighan, in the fourth chapter, provides a view of group decision making that departs from the two preceding chapters through its considerably stronger emphasis on social–psychological dynamics to explain group decision making. Rather than being concerned with how particular bits of information are weighted, combined, or recalled in the process of reaching a decision, Murnighan's concern, as illustrated in his model, is with how group decisions result from implicit and explicit use of decision rules (e.g., majority rule), the distribution of power among group members, and the behavior of group members as a function of these parameters. Murninghan provides an extensive account of input-oriented interventions designed to make groups more effective. These involve actions that are sometimes easily accomplished, such as minimizing group size and arranging the structure of payoffs to group members to facilitate group performance, yet they also involve some actions perhaps more difficult to accomplish, such as altering the perceptions of group members.

Hoffman's theoretical orientation, conveyed in the fifth chapter, is an encompassing one, dealing with both information-processing activities and social psychological dynamics. The latter receive greater emphasis in the discussions of norms, for example, and the former are addressed in terms of the accumulation of valence by alternatives considered by a group. It is interesting to compare a feature of Hoffman's chapter with a feature of the Hartwick, Sheppard, and Davis chapter, since each explicitly addresses the intersection of information-processing activities and social–psychological dynamics in group decision making, Hartwick and his coauthors discuss an information-processing activity (memory) as being influenced by social–psychological factors such as the presence or absence of others and the degree of bias in a group. Hoffman shows that the influence arrow can also be drawn in the other direction by indicating that certain social–psychological aspects of groups can be influenced by information-processing activities (namely, the accumulation of valence). Thus, the mutual influence of information-processing activities and social psychological dynamics in decision-making groups is made clear. Hoffman suggests that increased group decision-making effectiveness can be brought about by input-oriented interventions such as altering the trust level of groups (a point in concurrence with Murninghan) and composing the group properly. He also identifies action-oriented interventions to improve decision making, such as separating information getting from information evaluation, ways of acting to avoid assumed consensus, and the making explicit of norms and assumptions guiding group behavior. Methods for carrying out these interventions are discussed by Hoffman.

In the sixth chapter, it is clear that Stein's concern is at once both particular and universal. Creativity is examined as a process of great universality in human affairs, yet it is also treated as a process of particular relevance to decision-making groups. In this chapter, creativity is defined as an information-processing activity involving the transformation of existing ideas and their integration into a form not previously in existence. Stein addresses information processing at a molar level of analysis, unlike the more molecular analyses of Cook and Hammond and Hartwick, Sheppard, and Davis, and he goes on to identify many social–psychological influences on it, such as group norms and the aging, or maturation, of groups. Stein offers detailed information about composing groups to maximize creativity in decision making, an input-oriented intervention. Results of his analysis of the creative personality can be used to guide the composition of groups. He also mentions the value of action-oriented strategies of enhancing the creativity of decision-making groups.

References

Back, K. W. The small group tightrope between sociology and personality. *Journal of Applied Behavioral Science,* 1979, *15,* 283–294.

Bradford, L. P. Introduction. *Journal of Social Issues,* 1948, *4,* 2–7.

Cartwright, A., & Zander, A. (Eds.), *Group dynamics* (3rd ed.). New York: Harper and Row, 1968.

Delbecq, A. L., Van de Ven, A. H., & Gustafson, A. H. *Group techniques for program planning.* Glenview, Illinois: Scott, Foresman, 1975.

Eils, L. C., & John, R. S. A criterion validation of multiattribute utility analysis and of group communication strategy. *Organizational Behavior and Human Performance,* 1980, *25,* 268–288.

Gordon, K. Group judgments in the field of lifted weights. *Journal of Experimental Psychology,* 1924, *7,* 398–400.

Hall, J., & Watson, W. H. The effects of normative intervention on group decision-making performance. *Human Relations,* 1970, *23,* 299–317.

Hall, J., & Williams, M. S. Group dynamics training and improved decision making. *Journal of Applied Behavioral Science,* 1970, *6,* 39–68.

Hammond, K. R., Rohrbaugh, K., Mumpower, J., & Adelman, L. Social judgment theory: Applications in policy formation. *In* M. F. Kaplan & S. Schwartz (Eds.). *Human judgment and decision processes in applied settings.* New York: Academic Press, 1977.

Hoffman, L. R. Applying experimental research on group problem solving to organizations. *Journal of Applied Behavioral Science,* 1979, *15,* 375–391.

Janis, I. L. *Victims of groupthink.* Boston: Houghton-Mifflin, 1972.

Knight, H. C. A comparison of the reliability of group and individual judgments. Master's thesis, Columbia University, 1921. Cited in Lorge, I., Fox, D., Davitz, J., & Brenner, M. A survey of studies contrasting the quality of group performance and individual performance, 1920–1957. *Psychological Bulletin,* 1958, *55,* 337–372.

Maier, N. R. F. *Problem-solving discussions and conferences: Leadership methods and skills.* New York: McGraw-Hill, 1963.

Maier, N. R. F. *Problem solving and creativity: In individuals and groups.* Belmont, California: Brooks/Cole, 1970.

Schmuck, R. A., Runkel, P. J., & Langmeyer, A. Improving organizational problem solving in a school faculty. *Journal of Applied Behavioral Science,* 1969, *5,* 455–482.

Shaw, M. E. A comparison of individuals and small groups in the rational solution of complex problems. *American Journal of Psychology,* 1932, *44,* 491–504.

Slovic, P., Fischoff, B., & Lichtenstein, S. Behavioral decision theory. *In* M. R. Rosenzweig and L. W. Porter (Eds.), *Annual Review of Psychology* (Vol. 30). Palo Alto, California: Annual Reviews Inc., 1979.

Vroom, V. H., Grant, L. D., & Cotton, T. J. The consequences of social interaction in group problem solving. *Organizational Behavior and Human Performance,* 1969, *4,* 77–95.

Zander, A. The study of group behavior during four decades. *Journal of Applied Behavioral Science,* 1979, *15,* 272–282. (a)

Zander, A. The psychology of group processes. In M. R. Rosenzweig and L. W. Porter (Eds.), *Annual Review of Psychology* (Vol. 30). Palo Alto, California: Annual Reviews, 1979. (b)

2

Interpersonal Learning and Interpersonal Conflict Reduction in Decision-Making Groups[1,2]

RICHARD L. COOK
KENNETH R. HAMMOND

EDITOR'S INTRODUCTION

In this chapter, Cook and Hammond present a distinctive view of group decision making. The theoretical approach taken up is one that has long roots in the study of the judgment and inference processes of individuals, and it has only recently been extended into the domain of group decision making. It is an explicitly cognitive approach, one concerned with how individuals process information for decision making, giving particularly close attention to the ways in which people attach weights of importance to relevant considerations and the ways in which this information is combined to form a preference or decision. In the group decision-making setting, it is not only the operation of these cognitive processes that is of interest to this theoretical approach, but also the differences among group members in their weighing and combining of information. Many obstacles to decision making arise from these differences. These differences also spur much of the action of group

[1] Preparation of this chapter was supported in part by NSF Grant No. IST-7819867 "Designing Information Systems for More Effective Use in Decision Making."

[2] Correspondence regarding this article should be sent to Richard L. Cook, Center for Research on Judgment and Policy, Campus Box 485, University of Colorado, Boulder, Colorado 80309.

IMPROVING GROUP DECISION MAKING IN ORGANIZATIONS

Copyright © 1982 by Academic Press, Inc.
All rights of reproduction in any form reserved.
ISBN: 0-12-310980-9

*decision making, such as argumentation for and against alternative solutions
and attempts to reconcile divergent points of view.*

*As Cook and Hammond explain, group decision making can be improved
by providing group members, in explicit and succinct form, information
about how each is weighing and combining information in the establishment
of his or her own preferred decision alternative. The techniques of collecting
and presenting this information are described in this chapter, and it quickly
becomes apparent that these techniques are of a sophisticated yet widely
applicable nature. The many potentially beneficial consequences of these
techniques are discussed thoroughly by Cook and Hammond.*

Managers in modern organizations, both public and private, must make
difficult decisions requiring the integration of information from a variety of
sources. Computer technology has led to the development of large data
bases containing information about internal and external factors affecting
organizational performance, and data retrieval systems give the manager
access to unlimited routine and ad hoc reports derived from these sources.
Computer-based models of the organization are also used to study interactions between system components and to make projections of future growth
based on alternative assumptions and policies.

Unfortunately, improvements in technological capabilities have not been
matched by increases in our understanding of or our ability to aid the
decision-making process that the technology is meant to serve. In this chapter we will provide a remedy for this situation; we will describe how technology can be used to aid the decision-making process so that a decision
maker can learn about and better understand how he or she is making
decisions in a specific context. This approach can serve, moreover, as a basis
for helping decision makers to communicate with each other regarding complex policy issues. The technology thus becomes an aid to individual and
group decision making. Indeed, it forms the base for developing a Decision
Support System that goes beyond organizing and displaying information; it
supports the decision-making process itself.

A Decision Support System for Site Selection

In order to illustrate how computer aids to decision making can facilitate
interpersonal communication and conflict reduction in an organizational
context, we will describe an example of the application of such aids to the
problem of selecting sites for expansion by a company that operates
medium-sized neighborhood retail stores. The example shows how a

computer-based system could be developed to aid managers in selecting sites. The system encompasses both information about potential sites and a methodology for helping managers within the company improve the decision-making process. The use of a concrete example provides a realistic perspective for examining group decision making in the organizational context in which it takes place. Although the specific problem is hypothetical, it is similar in essential respects to a number of actual applications of the approach described here. Several of these applications are discussed after the site selection example is described in detail.

The selection of a site for a new retail store is a complex problem with important economic implications for the organization operating the store. A poorly chosen site for the store could result in its failure, while a good site should lead to economic success. The evaluation of a potential site as "good" or "bad" is, however, a judgment requiring an analysis of site characteristics in light of organizational policy. Many different characteristics of a site could, conceivably, be related to its potential as a location for a new store, but these characteristics would be imperfectly and unreliably related to the actual success or failure of a given store. That is, it would not be possible in practice to make a perfect prediction of relative success for alternative sites, but it is the goal company management will want to work toward by selecting those site characteristics that are the best predictors available.

The process of selecting characteristics to be considered in evaluating potential sites would depend, to some extent, on the past experience of the company. A company without past experience in selecting sites would have to depend on the judgment of the appropriate managers or other decision makers within the company to make such evaluations, although these judgments might be based in part on knowledge about the experience of similar kinds of companies in expanding into new markets.

As the company chooses sites and opens new stores, it will be possible to consider the relative success of those stores as new site selection decisions are made. Although it might take some time to properly determine the economic success of a store, company management would eventually have access to a data bank of information about store characteristics that could be statistically related to the economic performance of each store already in existence. Dependence on the judgment of the company's managers would, therefore, be reduced but not eliminated, since evaluations of success and statistical relationships derived from past experience would have to be adjusted to take into account such external factors as economic conditions in a specific community or the entry of unexpected competition. An excellent prediction, firmly grounded in past experience and wise judgment on the part of the manager, might still result in the selection of a site that results in failure because of external conditions over which the company has little control.

Organizational policy is also a critical aspect of site evaluation. It was assumed in the preceding discussion that assessing the success of a given store would be a straightforward task, yet this is unlikely to be true in practice. It might take some time, for example, to make an adequate determination of whether a particular store was successful economically, and even then the evaluation would have to allow for the role of such external factors as economic conditions in the community or the entry of unexpected competition. Unless there is a clearly defined organizational policy for making an evaluation of economic success, the company's managers will be left with an additional task requiring the exercise of their judgment in a complex and uncertain environment. Furthermore, the economic success or failure of a particular store would ordinarily be only one of the criteria company management would want to consider in evaluating existing and potential sites. Other factors of relevance might include a desire to enhance the company's image by expansion in a particular region, filling a gap in service coverage for the company's products, challenging a competitor who is expanding to a new geographic area, and so forth. Clearly, the relative importance of such factors could vary over time, and different companies would take different approaches to making such evaluations.

The situation typically found in many organizations is that planning decisions are left to managers on the assumption that these managers are, in fact, implementing organizational policy. The policy of the organization is usually only formulated in a vague and imprecise manner, however. Such verbal means of communication as memoranda and meetings are used to convey organizational policy but, as will be demonstrated, verbal communication is a highly fallible and unreliable means of describing something as complex as organizational policy. The most immediate symptom of this failure in communicating organizational policy is often the inability of managers at various levels within the department to articulate such a policy or to identify critical characteristics that could be used to determine the relative desirability of alternative sites. The first task, therefore, is to work with management to determine the characteristics of sites that are closely related to organizational goals.

Site Evaluation Characteristics

In developing a site selection system, it is important that the dimensions chosen to evaluate potential sites represent the interests, views, and contributions of different managers within the company in order to ensure the development of a comprehensive list of site characteristics. The specific list of characteristics would, of course, vary from company to company. The following are six characteristics typical of those that might be chosen by managers in a given company. The six characteristics are meant to be indicative of the different kinds of information that might be relevant to site selection decisions and they will be used as the basis of the decision support system described below.

Average Income: The average income of residents living within the geographic boundaries of a site would be related to the disposable income of the residents and to the anticipated dollar volume of the store. The relationship need not be a simple linear one, however. A manager in a company operating a chain of exclusive, and expensive, high fidelity stores might feel there is little difference between a site with a low average income and one with a moderate average income; both sites would be poor locations for one of the company's stores. As average income rises above a moderate level, however, this factor could be strongly related to the evaluation of alternative sites. The information about this characteristic would come directly from a commercial data base derived from census results. The range for this variable would be defined by the set of sites under consideration.

Average Age: The age of residents of a community or site could also be a potentially strong determinant of the likelihood of buying from a particular store. Many retailers would be most interested in young adults as possible customers and less interested in older or younger individuals, but the role of this factor might be highly dependent on the kind of store operated by the company. Needed data would again be obtained from a commercial data base with census information.

Proportion Who Commute: Unlike the preceding two variables, the proportion of people in a community who commute out of that community to work would be negatively related to the evaluation of that community as a potential site, since this would mean that some of the disposable income of residents would probably be spent elsewhere. Information about commuting habits should also be available from a commercial data base of site information.

Projected Population Growth: The success of an as yet unbuilt store will depend on future and not present conditions in a community. While many characteristics of a community can be expected to remain reasonably stable over moderate time spans, this may not be true of characteristics such as actual population. The population of some communities will remain stable while other communities will grow rapidly and some will even show decreases in population. The set of sites considered by the managers would probably have been selected so that only geographic areas with at least some minimal population would be considered further. Whereas actual population might not be of interest, the growth trend would be of considerable interest.

The growth trend could be determined by retrieving a series of population values over time for each site and fitting a growth curve to the data. The projected rate of growth for the time period of interest to the company would then become one of the factors used to evaluate sites. This characteristic would be described by a computed value—the result of applying a simple modeling technique to data from a data base.

Competition Rating: A company is not likely to locate a new retail store in an area without considering the kind of competition that would be encountered. The impact of such competition would depend on such factors as the number of competing stores, their relative size, the degree of overlap with products marketed by other stores, the actual location of other stores, and the likelihood of entry of new stores into the area. The degree of competition could be quite difficult to assess, but, because of its importance, should not be ignored. One approach to obtaining information about competition would be to have a marketing specialist visit each potential site and assign it a numerical rating after reviewing it in light of the previous considerations. The rating could be one of attractiveness of the site with respect to competitive positioning. The site evaluation would now include judgmental information based on the company's marketing expertise. Because this judgment is complex, it would be desirable to monitor its reliability by having more than one expert participate in evaluating sites. Disagreement among the experts would imply a need to decompose the problem in order to study how the experts are reaching their conclusions. The site evaluation problem would then become a hierarchical judgment task.

Market Survey: The final source of information about sites to be considered for purposes of this example is a market survey. In addition to the demographic data just described, company management would also like to have a more direct assessment of the attitudes of residents with respect to the company's products. The company might, therefore, do a preliminary screening of potential sites and then hire a survey research firm to do a telephone survey of the residents of promising sites. Survey results could be described in terms of overall favorableness of resident attitudes toward the company, and this information would be added to the data base of information about site characteristics.

The site data base, as developed for this example, contains a variety of kinds of information about potential sites, including objective census data, a statistical prediction based on a model of population growth, a subjective judgment of competition, and an attitudinal survey of site residents. Simply identifying relevant characteristics is an important first step in the development of a site selection policy, but leaves unanswered the question of how this information should be combined. To address this problem, it is first necessary to determine how individual managers use the information about site characteristics in evaluating individual sites and then to provide the managers with a means for communicating their evaluation policies to others and for arriving at an acceptable compromise policy for actual use in site selection. We will first discuss some of the difficulties that arise in attempting to communicate information about judgment policies and then turn to a description of a methodology for overcoming these difficulties.

Communication of Judgment Policies

Structuring a decision problem is an essential first step in solving the problem, since this step facilitates interaction and communication between the decision makers involved. Reaching a decision will ordinarily involve making trade-offs between the factors affecting the decision, and this is a difficult and poorly understood aspect of decision making. Research conducted over the past quarter century has demonstrated conclusively that people have a poor understanding of how they make such trade-offs (see Slovic & Lichtenstein, 1971, for a comprehensive review of such research). When asked to assign weights according to the relative importance of each factor, for example, people give subjective weights that bear only a rough resemblance to weights derived from a statistical analysis of actual decisions. One bias affecting such judgments is a tendency to distribute subjective weights over a large number of factors when, in a statistical sense, much less information is actually being used to arrive at a decision. This bias is quite stable and persists regardless of the method used to obtain subjective weights. Cook and Stewart (1975) compared seven different approaches to weight elicitation and found that all methods were equally poor when compared with statistical policy descriptions.

If decision makers have a poor understanding of their own judgment policies and are unable to describe these policies accurately, it is not surprising that communication between decision makers about complex issues is a highly fallible process often resulting in misunderstanding and conflict. Even if two decision makers agree in principle, they may well disagree in practice because of imperfect understanding of their own judgment policies.

The difficulty of communicating information about judgment policies was strikingly demonstrated in a study of labor–management negotiations conducted by Balke, Hammond, and Meyer (1973; see also Hammond, Cook, & Adelman, 1977). Balke and his associates worked with three labor and three management negotiators who had been involved in a long and costly strike at a chemical company. The negotiators were asked to reenact their positions at the conclusion of the strike (the study was done a few months later), and to work through an exercise in which they evaluated a series of possible contracts and also predicted the evaluations of their labor or management counterparts. Analyses of their judgments showed that the three labor negotiators held roughly similar positions with respect to the major issues, whereas the three management negotiators held three divergent positions. Furthermore, the negotiators on each side predicted poorly how the negotiators on the other side would evaluate the various contracts. The management negotiators, for example, assumed that the labor negotiators placed a high weight on salary; the salary issue had, however, been solved by the final days of the strike as far as labor was concerned, and the recall of strikers who had been laid off had become the most important issue to the labor negotiators.

Analyses of the judgments of the labor and management negotiators showed that the individual negotiators were inconsistent and unreliable in their evaluations of possible contracts and that they had done a poor job of communicating their policies to the others—despite months of discussion at the bargaining table. Also, the management negotiators failed to present a common front in the negotiations, since these three negotiators held markedly different policies.

If two people are to agree with respect to their judgments, they must agree about or be able to reach a compromise on principles and they must be able to make their judgments in a reliable, consistent manner. Analyses of the judgments of the labor and management negotiators suggested that the negotiators were inconsistent in making judgments and, partly as a consequence of this inconsistency, communicated their policies poorly. Although the negotiators from the two sides were not in complete agreement on the principles or issues on which the strike had focused, neither were the differences as great as had been imagined. The implication was that the strike could have been settled much earlier if the negotiators had had a better understanding of their own policies and had been better able to communicate these policies to the others.

SOCIAL JUDGMENT THEORY

The procedures used to demonstrate the inability of the labor and management negotiators to communicate or even to completely understand their judgment policies were based on an approach to cognition and social interaction referred to as Social Judgment Theory (SJT, see Hammond, Stewart, Brehmer, & Steinmann, 1975). The focus of this theory is on the difficulty inherent in the task of integrating complex, probabilistic information from a variety of sources in order to arrive at a decision.

Many examples of social conflict and interpersonal misunderstanding appear to be directly related to the cognitive complexity of the underlying judgment task. SJT provides a framework for analyzing the sources of conflict and misunderstanding and for providing decision makers with a methodology for overcoming these limitations.

In addition to the labor–management negotiations example previously described, SJT has been applied to a number of other problems of policy formation in both public and private organizations (see Hammond, Rohrbaugh, Mumpower, & Adelman, 1977). Examples have included the resolution of a dispute over the choice of handgun ammunition by the police department in a large city (Hammond & Adelman, 1976), the development of land use policies (e.g., Rohrbaugh & Wehr, 1978), providing improved methods for citizen participation in governmental policy formation (Stewart & Gelberd, 1976), and developing a planning framework for a research organization (Adelman, Stewart, & Hammond, 1975). The application of SJT to such problems has been facilitated by computer aids used to help decision makers understand their own policies and to communicate their policies to others. The development of such computer aids is discussed next.

COMPUTER-AIDED JUDGMENT ANALYSIS

If decision makers find it difficult to describe their judgment policies or to apply their policies in a consistent manner, what is needed is an aid to help decision makers overcome these limitations. SJT, the basis of the previous discussion of inconsistency and conflict, also suggests a methodology for analyzing the judgments of a decision maker and for communicating information about the decision maker's judgment policy to the decision maker and to others. A plausible model of how a person arrives at a complex judgment involving trade-offs between multiple factors is that he or she assesses the value or level on each factor for each object or alternative in question and then combines this information according to the importance of each factor.

A statistical technique that closely approximates the characteristics of this model is multiple regression analysis. Regression analysis allows one to determine the relationships between a set of intercorrelated dimensions and a criterion variable—in this case, the judgments made by a decision maker. The results of the analyses provide statistical weights indicative of the relative importance of each dimension to the decision maker. A measure of the predictability of the decision maker's judgments, the multiple correlation coefficient, is also obtained. A high multiple correlation coefficient suggests that the decision maker's judgments are being modeled quite accurately, while a low coefficient suggests either that the model is inaccurate or that the decision maker is making judgments in an unreliable, inconsistent manner. In the case of a low coefficient, further analyses can be performed to determine whether error in the model or low reliability is the source of problem.

It is important to note that the use of multiple regression analysis to model a decision maker's judgment policy is not meant to imply that the decision maker actually uses a mental equation to compute his or her judgments. Rather the regression analysis is meant to be a useful representation of what the decision maker tries to do when faced with the task of making trade-offs among multiple, interrelated factors in arriving at a judgment. The resulting model can be said to be a paramorphic representation of how the decision maker arrives at a judgment (Hoffman, 1960); the structure of the model is similar to that of the cognitive process even though the calculational methods may differ.

One implication of the previous argument is that in those situations where it is reasonable to assume that a decision maker is arriving at a judgment by making trade-offs among the dimensions of a problem according to their relative importance, the decision maker's judgment may be unreliable and inconsistent because of the lack of a computational aid. It would appear that this is often the case. Studies of models of decision making have shown, almost without exception, that the model outperforms the decision maker (Dawes, 1979; Goldberg, 1970; Meehl, 1954). That is, if a set of judgments made by a decision maker is analyzed and the statistical model is then used to make predictions of those judgments, the predictions are a better predictor of an external criterion. The computer applies the statistical model with perfect consistency, of course. A most important and unexpected result is that the improvement in consistency is ordinarily more important than any error or bias in the modeling process.

Most of the research referred to previously has depended on retrospective analyses of a decision maker's judgments. Interactive computer facilities now make it possible, however, for the development of a model of a person's judgment policy to be a collaborative process in which the decision maker can review the statistical description of his or her policy, including the judgments predicted by the model, and modify or revise the policy description as necessary (see Cook, 1980).

In the next section, the development of a model of an individual's judgment policy will be described in detail, using the site selection problem as context. Such individual policy descriptions will then provide a framework for group interaction and communication, leading to the development of a compromise company policy for site selection.

Developing a Project Prioritization Policy

POLICY is an interactive computer program that can be used to present a series of profiles to a decision maker for evaluation and then to analyze the decision maker's judgments and to present graphical displays describing the decision maker's judgment policy. The profiles represent examples of the decision problem or task and the decision maker ordinarily is asked to evaluate each profile on a numerical scale to indicate overall desirability, utility, expected performance, or some similar measure. A prospective home buyer might, for example, be shown information about the size, location, price, and other features of a house and be asked to judge its desirability; a member of a college admissions committee could be shown test scores, grade-point average, and ratings of letters of recommendation for an applicant and be asked to predict college performance; or a politician might be shown the impact of a tax proposal in terms of its effects on various subgroups in the population and be asked to rate the political acceptability of the proposal.

Two examples of profiles depicting possible alternative locations for new stores are shown in Figure 2.1. The sites are described in terms of the six dimensions elicited from the company's management. For each site, the level on each dimension is shown as a bar graph represented by a row of Xs on the computer terminal. This form of graphical display is often used in applications of interactive judgment analysis because it is easy for the decision maker to evaluate and respond to such displays. It is important, however, that the task dimensions and end-points be clearly and unambiguously defined, particularly if more than one decision maker participates. The POLICY program can also display either numerical values for each characteristic or not display profile information at all. In the latter case, other forms of display, such as slides, overhead transparencies, or booklets, could be used to present the profiles, while the computer terminal would be used only for entry of the decision maker's judgments. These alternative display formats, while requiring more time and effort to prepare, would allow for more natural forms of profile presentation in some situations.

The first site (CASE 1) displayed can be seen to have a very high competition rating, moderately high average income, a very low proportion of people who commute, and intermediate levels on the other characteristics. The second site has a higher average age and projected population growth and results of the market survey are more favorable, while the proportion of people who commute is still low and ratings on the two other factors have declined. Each manager evelutes a series of site profiles. In this example, a 10-point rating scale has been used and the first site has been given a relatively low evaluation of 4, whereas the second site has been given a moderately high evaluation of 8.

The manager in this example prefers the second site to the first, but it is not clear from the examination of only two judgments how the decision maker is weighting each factor and combining the information about site characteristics in order to arrive at an overall evaluation. Once a series of site evalua-

```
CASE 1                              ...........

AVERAGE INCOME                      XXXXXXX

AVERAGE AGE                         XXXXX

PROP. WHO COMMUTE                   X

PROJ. POP. GROWTH                   XXXX

COMPETITION RATING                  XXXXXXXXX

MARKET SURVEY                       XXXXX
                                    ...........
EVALUATION?    4



CASE 2                              ...........

AVERAGE INCOME                      XXXX

AVERAGE AGE                         XXXXXXXX

PROP. WHO COMMUTE                   XX

PROJ. POP. GROWTH                   XXXXXX

COMPETITION RATING                  XXXXX

MARKET SURVEY                       XXXXXXXX
                                    ...........
EVALUATION?    8
```

Figure 2.1. Computer-generated displays of two alternative profiles of site characteristics. Using a 10-point scale, the decision maker has given the second site a higher evaluation.

tions has been obtained, however, the POLICY program can be instructed to perform statistical analyses of the decision maker's judgments and to display the results of the analyses to the decision maker. A graphical display showing the predictability of the decision maker's judgments and the proportional weight placed on each factor is shown in Figure 2.2. The predictability is a multiple correlation coefficient with a maximum value of 1.0. A value of 0.91 is high and suggests that the statistical model of how this manager is making site evaluations is a good one.

The relative weights shown in Figure 2.2 have been derived from statistical regression weights (see Hammond, Stewart, Brehmer, & Steinmann,

```
POLICY 'EVALUATION' HAS A PREDICTABILITY OF 0.91

RELATIVE WEIGHT PROFILE


A:   EVALUATION

0.0----------0.5----------1.0        WEIGHT    FUNCT FORM
AVERAGE INCOME
AAAAA                                 0.14      POSLIN


AVERAGE AGE
AAAA                                  0.11      NONLIN


PROP. WHO COMMUTE
AAA                                   0.08      NEGLIN


PROJ. POP. GROWTH
AAAAAAAAA                             0.27      NONLIN


COMPETITION RATING
AAAAA                                 0.16      NONLIN


MARKET SURVEY
AAAAAAAA                              0.24      POSLIN

0.0----------0.5----------1.0
```

Figure 2.2.   A display of the relative statistical weights derived from an analysis of the decision maker's evaluations.

1975), and for ease of presentation and discussion have been adjusted to sum to 1.0 so that they can be interpreted as the proportional influence or importance of each dimension. The highest weights for this manager are on projected population growth and the results of the market survey. Other characteristics are of moderate importance. It should be emphasized that the display of relative weights is a statistical description of how the manager made a series of judgments and not a prescription of how the manager ought to make such judgments. The display is a tool designed to improve the manager's understanding of how he or she is making judgments and the ability to communicate that information to others. Procedures that allow the decision maker to modify the policy description and to evaluate the implications of alternative policies are discussed later.

In addition to the relative importance of each dimension, it is useful to know how the individual dimensions are related to the decision maker's overall evaluation. At a very gross level, we would want to know whether the decision maker feels that more or less of a given characteristic is desirable. In the site evaluation example, all factors would presumably be positively related to the site evaluation of any rational manager (if the dimension is given any weight at all), with the possible exceptions of the proportion who commute and average age. As was noted earlier, the proportion of residents who commute would probably be a negative factor in a manager's evaluations because of the greater likelihood that some disposable income would be spent outside of the geographic boundaries of the site. The manner in which average age would be related to site evaluations is more difficult to predict and would depend on the kind of store operated by the company.

The relative weight profile (Figure 2.2) indicates that the relationships between two of the site characteristics, average income and market survey results, are positive and linear (POSLIN), while one functional relationship, the proportion who commute, is negative and linear (NEGLIN), and the other relationships are nonlinear (NONLIN). Figure 2.3 shows a computer-generated display of the functional relationship between each of the site characteristics and the manager's evaluations. In this display, the height of each function form has been adjusted to reflect the relative weight placed on each factor. The nonlinear function form for average age shows that the manager prefers sites with a moderately high average age, while sites with older residents are not as desirable and sites with a low average age are least desirable. The function form for projected population growth, on the other hand, is approximately positive and linear, although the manager does not see much difference between sites that are moderately low or very low on this factor. In contrast, the function form for the competition rating levels off, suggesting that the manager would like a site to have at least an average rating on this characteristic but is indifferent to increases beyond that level.

ITERATIVE POLICY ANALYSIS

One advantage to using an interactive computer program to develop and display a model of a decision maker's judgment policy is that the decision maker can be shown the description of the model immediately and can also evaluate alternative analyses or even make changes in the policy description. The POLICY program includes a large number of options for performing alternative analyses or for revising a policy description and seeing the implications of those revisions. The decision maker can, for example, make changes in the relative weights and then review computer-generated predicted evaluations for each of the profiles.

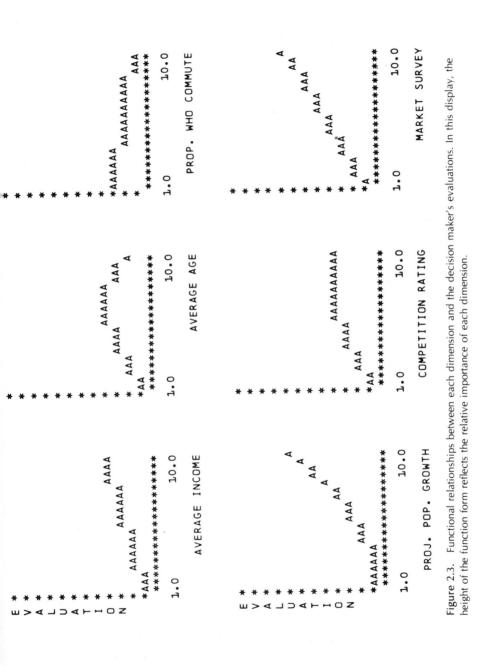

Figure 2.3. Functional relationships between each dimension and the decision maker's evaluations. In this display, the height of the function form reflects the relative importance of each dimension.

27

```
POLICY 'REVISED' HAS A PREDICTABILITY OF 1.00

RELATIVE WEIGHT PROFILE


A:   REVISED

0.0-----------0.5-----------1.0        WEIGHT    FUNCT FORM

AVERAGE INCOME

AAAAA                                    0.15      POSLIN


AVERAGE AGE

AAA                                      0.10      NONLIN


PROP. WHO COMMUTE

AAA                                      0.10      NEGLIN


PROJ. POP. GROWTH

AAAAAAAA                                 0.25      POSLIN


COMPETITION RATING

AAAAA                                    0.15      NONLIN


MARKET SURVEY

AAAAAAAA                                 0.25      POSLIN

0.0-----------0.5-----------1.0
```

Figure 2.4.   A relative weight profile for the revised weights specified directly by the decision maker. The evaluations of each profile that would be predicted by this policy could also be examined.

An example of a modified policy (REVISED) is shown in Figure 2.4. The manager has made slight adjustments to the relative weights assigned to each factor. The manager has also decided that the function form for the competition rating should not level off and it has been changed to positive and linear (shown as POSLIN in the weights display). The revised policy is, in effect, a mathematical equation, and its predictability is therefore perfect (1.0).

The manager can work iteratively with the policy description at the computer terminal, reviewing the implications of changes and making further revisions until he or she is satisfied with the policy description. A variety of complex function forms, or rules for combining information about the dimensions, can be considered if necessary. Most of these steps would be performed with hypothetical data or a subset of actual data as a matter of convenience. Once the decision maker is satisfied with the policy description, however, the process of applying the policy to actual cases can be automatic. The manager who is developing a site selection policy may have a large number of sites to evaluate. If the ratings of each site on each of the policy dimensions are stored in a computer data base, the statistical model of the manager's policy can be used to calculate a computed evaluation for each site. This was done for the policy of the manager described previously, using a demonstration data base containing site information and descriptions of the 10 best sites are shown in Figure 2.5. In this way, the policy cannot only be applied to an arbitrarily large number of sites, a task the manager could not perform in a reliable manner even if time were available for such a tedious task, but it can also be applied automatically to new sites, without the intervention of the manager, as they are entered into the data base. The site selection data base might, for example, be updated as new survey results or site evaluations are received, or it might be expanded to encompass new geographic regions as the company expands. Revised lists of the most desirable locations could be generated as needed.

The fact that the manager's policy description is stored in the computer does not, of course, imply that the policy will or should remain unchanged over time. One circumstance that might lead to a revision of the policy description would be changing external conditions, such as the national economic climate. A manager's policy for site selection might be more aggressive if economic conditions are favorable and more conservative if conditions are not favorable. In terms of the policy description shown previously, the manager might be less concerned about the level of competition in a given area, and therefore put less weight on that factor, if economic conditions are relatively favorable. It is even conceivable that a manager would seek out sites where there is strong competition if an aggressive marketing posture is seen as desirable during a time when the economy is strong.

Another circumstance that might lead to changes in the manager's policy would be the need to apply that policy to new situations. The site selection policy could be quite different for different regions of the country and the manager could develop new policies for the evaluation of sites as the company expands its operations. The manager might then have several policies stored in the computer at one time, including alternative policies for different contingencies or applications.

A final circumstance that would be expected to lead to revisions in the manager's policy would be experience with the application of a policy. As stores are built in new areas, the relative success of the stores would be information that could be added to the data base and related to the criteria originally used by the manager to select the sites for those stores. This objec-

POLICY 'REVISED'

COMPUTED RATING	SITE #	INCOME	AGE	COMMUTE	GROWTH	COMPETITION	SURVEY
9.7	SITE 30	10	2	1	5	8	9
9.0	SITE 34	3	7	5	7	10	9
8.4	SITE 40	8	3	7	6	8	9
8.2	SITE 47	5	1	9	9	8	10
7.8	SITE 15	8	8	8	9	7	4
7.7	SITE 18	3	9	3	5	5	10
7.4	SITE 7	5	5	5	8	1	9
6.6	SITE 17	5	10	5	7	4	7
6.3	SITE 38	6	10	6	7	9	4
6.2	SITE 29	4	6	2	2	7	9

Figure 2.5. A rank-ordered list of sites that have been evaluated by applying the decision maker's revised policy to the data base of site descriptions. The computed site evaluation is shown in the left column.

tive evidence could be incorporated into the manager's policy and the net effect would be to move toward a more analytical and less subjective policy for evaluating sites. In a static business environment, a completely objective model might eventually be developed, leaving the manager with time to move on to other problems requiring the exercise of his or her judgment— such as defining the dimensions needed to evaluate "success" and developing a policy for making such evaluations.

Group Policy Development

The approach to helping an individual develop a model of his or her judgment policy that was described previously is a powerful aid both to understanding and communication. It provides decision makers with a framework for understanding how judgments are made and this framework can help the decision maker describe the decision-making process to others. The graphical displays provided by the POLICY program can also, of course, be used as an aid to communication.

The displays of relative weights and function forms discussed previously are the primary aids used to help a decision maker achieve a better understanding of his or her judgment policy and to communicate information about that judgment policy to others. Often only the weights display is needed, since nonlinear functional relationships can usually be approximated by positive or negative linear function forms. The advantage of linear function forms is that the resulting policy is both easier to understand and to describe to others.

Although there are a number of different ways in which computer-aided judgment analysis can be used to facilitate group communication and policy development, a common first step is to work with group members to define the essential dimensions or characteristics of the problem being considered. This may be done in a meeting with all group members, or a few of the group members can develop a preliminary set of dimensions for review and evaluation by others. It is important to be relatively inclusive at this stage of the process, since it is easier to delete dimensions that turn out to be unimportant than to add dimensions that were forgotten. Nevertheless, as with a judgment analysis exercise with an individual decision maker, the list of dimensions is only tentative and subject to revision by the group members. What will be changed most frequently in actual applications are the definitions of the dimensions. It is important, however, to have a very explicit set of initial definitions so that group members have a common basis for their evaluations.

The next step in the group judgment analysis exercise, then, would be to have individuals make a series of evaluations of scenarios or profiles describing the judgment problem. These profiles might be presented in booklets, or each group member might work through an interactive session at the computer terminal as discussed previously. The mode of presentation will depend on such factors as the number of members in the group, access to computer facilities, and the importance and complexity of the problem. In the case of the site selection example, a small group of managers would be involved and the policy would be important to the company; the time and effort required to work through interactive sessions with individual managers would, therefore, be justified.

COMPARING THE POLICIES OF GROUP MEMBERS

When groups of managers or other decision makers with common interests participate in a judgment analysis exercise such as has been described here, the typical finding is that the individual policies are at least roughly similar. In particular, functional relationships are usually comparable, since if one person feels that more (or less) of a given characteristic is desirable, other decision makers are likely to feel the same way. Decision makers with common interests are not likely to be diametrically opposed on such issues (although methods for dealing with extreme disagreement follow).

Where decision makers in groups are likely to differ is with respect to the relative weights placed on the dimensions of the problem. Even here disagreement is often moderate. The research that has demonstrated the increased reliability of models of judgment processes when compared to actual judgments has also suggested that decision makers are good at defining the dimensions of a problem to be used for evaluation. Since decision makers typically agree on the dimensions to be considered, it is not surprising that any individual decision maker will probably put at least a moderate weight on each dimension chosen by the group.

Another frequent result of group interaction in specifying problem dimensions is that group members who may have been focusing on one or two characteristics of the problem are made aware of the relevance of other dimensions of the problem. A manager who had focused on projected population growth in evaluating sites for new stores might have overlooked the potential importance of the average income of residents in the area. As different managers contribute to the definition of the problem, individual managers become aware of other dimensions needed to adequately characterize the task and the relative weights placed on the dimensions are likely to become more evenly distributed.

The next step in facilitating group communication and conflict management is, then, to show managers where they agree and disagree with respect to their policies. The displays of relative weights and function forms can now be used to provide a graphical means of comparing policies. If the function forms are roughly comparable, then it is helpful to simplify the displays shown to the manager and a relative weight display comparing the policies of two or more decision makers can be used. An example of such a display for two of the managers who are addressing the site selection problem is shown in Figure 2.6. The two managers have somewhat different relative

```
POLICY 'MANAGER A' HAS A PREDICTABILITY OF 0.91

POLICY 'MANAGER B' HAS A PREDICTABILITY OF 0.82

RELATIVE WEIGHT PROFILE


A:   MANAGER A

B:   MANAGER B

0.0----------0.5-----------1.0        WEIGHT     FUNCT FORM

AVERAGE INCOME
AAAAA                                  0.14       POSLIN
BBBBBBB                                0.21       POSLIN

AVERAGE AGE
AAAA                                   0.11       NONLIN
BBBBB                                  0.14       NONLIN

PROP. WHO COMMUTE
AAA                                    0.08       NEGLIN
BBBBBB                                 0.19       NEGLIN

PROJ. POP. GROWTH
AAAAAAAAA                              0.27       NONLIN
BBBBB                                  0.16       POSLIN

COMPETITION RATING
AAAAA                                  0.16       NONLIN
BBBB                                   0.12       NONLIN

MARKET SURVEY
AAAAAAAA                               0.24       POSLIN
BBBBBB                                 0.18       POSLIN

0.0----------0.5-----------1.0
```

Figure 2.6. A display comparing the relative weights for two managers who have evaluated a series of possible sites for company expansion.

weights and the judgments of the second manager are less predictable by the model of judgment policy. It would be desirable to work through another series of sites with the second manager in order to determine whether an improved policy description could be obtained.

The two managers whose policies are shown in Figure 2.6 might now want to turn to an attempt to resolve the differences between their policies so that a compromise policy that would be used for actual site selection could be developed. Before discussing how this might be done, however, it is necessary to examine whether moderate policy differences of this magnitude have any practical consequences with respect to site selection.

WHEN DO POLICY DIFFERENCES MAKE A DIFFERENCE?

The results of the judgment analyses for decision-making groups typically show, as noted previously, that there are not only broad similarities between the policies of group members but also definite differences between some of the members with respect to the amount of weight placed on each factor. While these differences are of interest in themselves and usually provoke a considerable amount of policy-related discussion, such discussion is largely academic, since knowledge about the policy differences tells us little about the practical consequences of using different policies to make actual decisions.

To illustrate the preceding point, it is helpful to consider an example of a case of conflict that is more extreme than is ordinarily found in actual applications. Two managers with different views about how the company should grow and expand might, for example, have quite different opinions about the role of expansion into markets where there would be a high degree of competition—one manager would place a high positive weight on the rating of existing competition while the other manager would place a high negative weight on this factor. While it is quite likely that these two managers will engage in verbal disputes (and laboratory research confirms that this is so), the marked policy differences might not lead to different site evaluations. This could be true if all of the sites being evaluated were approximately equal with respect to the nature of the competition or if differences in the degree of competition were overshadowed by ratings on other factors.

This hypothetical example of conflict could, of course, have quite unfortunate consequences. The two managers might spend a considerable amount of time and energy discussing and arguing about the desirability of direct challenges to competitors even though their disagreement over this issue might be of little or no practical consequence. This situation occurs all too frequently; people engage in disputes without understanding the implications of the issues about which they are arguing.

It should be clear that providing managers with an aid that helps them understand their own policies and communicate those policies to others is an important first step but does not provide a complete system for helping managers improve the quality of their decisions. Managers also need to be shown the practical consequences of applying their policies in the context of the conditions that actually exist in the business environment within which they must operate. The implications of differences between policies must also be demonstrated in the context of this environment. Decision makers should focus their conflict resolution efforts on issues that make a difference. To do so requires information both about policies and about the characteristics of the problem being addressed.

The results of applying two different policies to two different data bases of site information are shown in Figures 2.7a and 2.7b. Figure 2.7a illustrates what might be referred to as a favorable situation, in that the pattern of ratings of sites on individual factors leads to only minimal conflict when the two policies are applied to the data to determine site selection decisions. Note, for example, that the highest ranked site for Policy A, Project 10, is the second-ranked site when Policy B is used. The top site for Policy B is ranked third by Policy A. Clearly these two managers would, in general, agree about

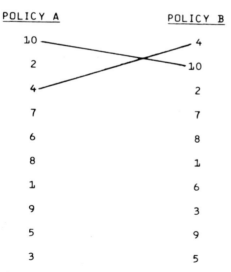

Figure 2.7a. Favorable conditions promoting agreement. Ten sites are ranked in order of preference as determined by applying the policies of two different managers to the ratings of each site on each dimension. Although there were moderate differences between the two policies with respect to the weight given to each dimension, the rank orders are quite similar and the two decision makers would tend to agree on site evaluations. Correlations between ratings of sites on each dimension were moderately positive in this case.

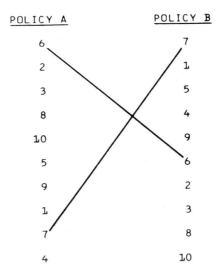

POLICY A	POLICY B
6	7
2	1
3	5
8	4
10	9
5	6
9	2
1	3
7	8
4	10

Figure 2.7b. Unfavorable conditions leading to conflict. The same two policies have been applied to ratings of a new set of sites for which the correlations between the dimensions were moderately negative. The rank orders of the sites are now quite different and the two decision makers would be in sharp disagreement over the evaluations of these sites.

how to evaluate this set of sites. The minor differences that do exist should be readily resolved and are not likely to be worth arguing about. The two managers should also be able to arrive at a compromise policy that could be used to determine site evaluations in the future.

When the same policies are applied to a different set of site descriptions, however, the results are much less favorable and there is considerable disagreement about site evaluations (Figure 7b). The top site for Policy A (Project 6) is now sixth for Policy B while the top site for Policy B is next to last on the rank-ordered list for A. Even though the same policies have been used, characteristics of the sites have changed and two managers holding these policies would be in sharp disagreement over how to evaluate sites even though they have not changed their evaluation policies. The only difference between the two sets of sites is that for the first set the correlations between dimensions are moderately high and positive while for the second set the correlations are also moderately high but negative.

Combining information about policies and information about sites yields, therefore, a complete picture of the evaluation problem showing not only where policy differences exist but also whether these differences are of any practical consequence. As the preceding example illustrates, the policies of the decision makers must be applied to the set of items or objects for which evaluations are actually desired if the implications of the differences between policies are to be examined. For the site selection task this would require use of the actual sites stored in the data base and policy descriptions would be applied to the values on each dimension for each of the sites. Correlations between dimensions for all sites would provide preliminary evidence as to whether agreement or disagreement between decision makers would be expected. High positive correlations would imply that moderate policy differences, such as those illustrated in Figure 2.6, would not have a major effect when the policies are applied to compute predicted evaluations; the decision makers would, therefore, tend to agree about their evaluations. Negative correlations between dimensions could mean that there would be considerable disagreement despite moderate policy differences.

Once the completed evaluations have been obtained it is possible, therefore, to evaluate the practical implications of the policy differences. A preliminary measure of agreement would be a correlation coefficient computed for each pair of decision makers. High correlations would indicate agreement and if more than two decision makers are involved the patterns of agreement between decision makers would be examined. Cluster analysis could also be used to determine what groups of individuals have similar policies.

Developing a Compromise Policy

Company management will ordinarily want to develop a single evaluation policy for making actual site selection decisions or recommendations. The graphical descriptions of individual judgment policies and the use of sensitivity analyses to show where policy differences have practical significance will often lead to a resolution of differences and an agreement on a compromise policy that is acceptable to the managers. Judgment analysis is a powerful aid to communication that allows management to address complex policy problems that might otherwise result in verbal disputes and a poor understanding and implementation of organizational policy.

Because judgment analysis is a descriptive aid to understanding and communication, its use does not guarantee that an acceptable compromise policy will be found. Even if an acceptable compromise cannot be achieved, however, the application of judgment analysis will lead to an improved understanding by managers of the sources of disagreement. Disagreement may, in turn, suggest a need for improved information about the relationship between site characteristics and selections. If managers disagree about the relationship between average age and site desirability, for example, this would suggest that additional information about the influence of this factor should be gathered, either from a market research firm with experience in site selection or by monitoring the role of this factor over time as new sites are selected.

Components of the Decision Support System

The Decision Support System (DSS) that was developed to help management solve the site selection problem encompasses a methodology for eliciting and communicating the evaluation policies of managers and a data base of information about sites. The creation or utilization of a data base of task-related information would, of course, be typical of most DSSs. Many such systems would also include models or simulation techniques to allow the manager to study the interactions between system components and to perform various "What if?" analyses. What is unusual about the DSS described here is the inclusion of an aid to help managers explicate their judgment policies regarding the trade-offs to be made in evaluating potential sites.

The approach to analyzing complex policy problems which has been described here is quite general and can be applied to any decision problem requiring trade-offs among dimensions of the task. An individual decision maker may be involved or there may be many decision makers and the task may require a single decision or a series of decisions. Judgment analysis can provide managers with a means for improving their understanding of their own judgment policies and for communicating this information to others. The explicit descriptions of judgment policies can provide, in turn, a basis for improved interpersonal understanding and conflict management.

The central role of the judgment analysis methodology in the design of a DSS is underscored by its influence on the other components of such a system. The data base, for example, might well include information about sites that the managers would never have thought to gather prior to structuring the problem in terms of the trade-offs inherent in site selection decisions.

Policy Support Systems

Management and computer scientists have developed an impressive array of tools for helping decision makers organize and manage information, including sophisticated data base systems and optimization models. Most complex policy problems require, however, an integration of such factual information and the values, goals, and preferences of decision makers. These values are imprecise, poorly understood, and difficult to communicate to others. The technology that has been described here encompasses an interactive computer system that is used (a) to externalize and communicate value functions; (b) to provide needed factual information and projections; and (c) to allow for an integration of facts and values. The system also provides a tracking and feedback mechanism that can be used to assess sensitivity to changes in assumptions about either factual information or the values of the managers.

The DSS that has been described here might better be referred to as a Policy Support System because it can be used not only to help organize and manage the flow of information regarding existing and planned sites, but also to provide managers with a framework for assessing and communicating their judgment policies. The system addresses, therefore, the entire policy process, including questions of fact and of value.

Current approaches to complex policy problems, on the other hand, are frequently inadequate and fail, not because of disagreement about questions of fact, but because of real or assumed disagreements over values. Current solutions to these problems focus on differences in personality, management style, or motivation, although the evidence from both research and experience suggests that such solutions do not succeed; indeed, they are apt to lead to continued conflict and misunderstanding because people are unskilled in communicating their judgment policies. They do not know how to form a judgment policy, what it should consist of, or how to describe it.

Policy making should focus on *thinking,* including an explication of cognitive processes. It should be supported by a system that will help people understand and communicate these processes. Such a decision support system was described in this chapter.

References

Adelman, L., Stewart, T. R., & Hammond, K. R. A case history of the application of social judgment theory to policy formulation. *Policy Sciences,* 1975, 6, 137–159.

Balke, W. M., Hammond, K. R., & Meyer, G. D. An alternative approach to labor–management relations. *Administrative Science Quarterly,* 1973, 18, 311–327.

Cook, R. L. Brunswik's Lens Model and the development of interactive judgment analysis. In K. R. Hammond & N. E. Wascoe (Eds.), *New directions for methodology of social and behavioral science: Realizations of Brunswik's representative design.* San Francisco: Jossey-Bass, 1980.

Cook, R. L., & Stewart, T. R. A comparison of seven methods for obtaining subjective descriptions of judgmental policy. *Organizational Behavior and Human Performance,* 1975, 13, 31–45.

Dawes, R. M. The robust beauty of improper linear models in decision making. *American Psychologist,* 1979, 34, 571–582.

Goldberg, L. R. Man versus model of man: A rationale, plus some evidence, for a method of improving on clinical inferences. *Psychological Bulletin,* 1970, 73, 422–432.

Hammond, K. R., & Adelman, L. Science, values, and human judgment. *Science,* 1976, *194,* 389–396.

Hammond, K. R., Cook, R. L., & Adelman, L. POLICY: An aid for decision making and international communication. *Columbia Journal of World Business,* 1977, *12,* 79–93.

Hammond, K. R., Rohrbaugh, J., Mumpower, J., & Adelman, L. Social judgment theory: Applications in policy formation. *In* M. F. Kaplan & S. Schwartz (Eds.), *Human judgment and decision processes in applied settings.* New York: Academic Press, 1977.

Hammond, K. R., Stewart, T. R., Brehmer, B., & Steinmann, D. O. Social judgment theory. *In* M. F. Kaplan & S. Schwartz (Eds.), *Human judgment and decision processes.* New York: Academic Press, 1975.

Hoffman, P. L. The paramorphic representation of clinical judgment. *Psychological Bulletin,* 1960, *67,* 116–131.

Meehl, P. E. *Clinical versus statistical prediction.* Minneapolis: University of Minnesota Press, 1954.

Rohrbaugh, J., & Wehr, P. Judgment analysis in policy formation: A new method for improving public participation. *Public Opinion Quarterly,* 1978, *42,* 521–532.

Slovic, P., & Lichtenstein, S. Comparison of Bayesian and regression approaches to the study of information processing judgment. *Organizational Behavior and Human Performance,* 1971, *6,* 649–744.

Stewart, T. R., & Gelberd, L. Analysis of judgment policy: A new approach for citizen participation in planning. *American Institute of Planners Journal,* 1976, *42,* 33–41.

Group Remembering:
Research and Implications

JON HARTWICK
BLAIR H. SHEPPARD
JAMES H. DAVIS

EDITOR'S INTRODUCTION

As Hartwick, Sheppard, and Davis point out at the opening of this chapter, considerable effort has been devoted to understanding processes of memory in the analysis of individual behavior, yet comparatively little attention has been given to the study of memory processes in the analysis of group behavior, especially with regard to group decision making. This chapter redresses that deficiency. It brings together the results of studies new and old about group remembering, gives us a view of the state of our knowledge about this phenomenon, and discusses the implications of this knowledge for the practice of decision making.

The tack adopted by Hartwick, Sheppard, and Davis describes group memory in terms of the component processes used to describe individual memory: acquisition, retention, and recall. Beyond this descriptive framework, however, the study of individual and group memory part company. In the latter, as this chapter shows, the concern is with understanding the ways in which social psychological factors (such as audience effects and the exposure to the presentation of information by fellow group members) affects these component processes of memory and the consequences of these effects for group performance. Further, models of group remembering are vastly different from those of individual remembering. Two competing models of

IMPROVING GROUP DECISION MAKING IN ORGANIZATIONS

group remembering are examined in this chapter. One is of "truth wins" nature, according to which group remembering is a function of the correctness of the information and a minimum number of individuals recalling it, and the other a majority rule process of remembering. Group remembering is a phenomenon of importance to the performance of many group tasks, especially decision making. The chapter concludes by discussing the implications of what is known about group remembering for decision-making effectiveness.

Most recent theories of individual-level decision making, or problem solving, have emphasized the acquisition, retention, recall, and treatment of information relevant to the decision. In fact, several prominent organizational theorists have suggested that the individual's relatively small capacity to process decision-relevant information is usually the limiting factor in the quality of most decisions (e.g., March & Simon, 1958). In industry, the technique most often used to improve the nature of the decision process in situations requiring the processing of a large amount of information is to establish a work, problem, task, planning, or decision group. Thus, it is quite surprising that very little is known about how groups acquire, store, and remember information (for similar views, see Cattell, 1953; Davis, 1969). The purpose of this chapter will be to review the small amount of social psychological research on information acquisition, storage, and retrieval in groups, discuss its implications for the question of group effectiveness, and suggest some directions that further research could take.

Our interest in group remembering arose from casual observations of the information-processing behavior of mock juries in studies conducted over a period of several years at the University of Illinois (see Davis, 1980a, for a summary). Until now, this research has emphasized, perhaps disproportionately, the group verdict itself over the manner in which juries treat trial information to reach such a verdict. In any event, experimenters in these studies noticed a number of recurring events that seemed to limit the group's effectiveness in dealing with information. Two typical scenarios should serve to illustrate how our interest came about.

1. The group often seemed to fumble in search of a critical piece of evidence in the case; after some time, one of the members would firmly assert what the nature of the critical evidence was. This individual was often wrong. However, the group would often accept that assertion as fact, and, in addition, the individual providing the information thereafter acquired expert status—arbitrating debates over not only evidence, but also interpretations of law and differences of opinion.

2. Some mock juries appeared to adopt attitudes, such that, over time, individual jurors would increasingly recall information consistent with one side of the case and suppress information consistent with the opposing position. At the point of decision, the evidence would then often appear to strongly support one side.

Interestingly, these phenomena typically resulted in two sets of juries in our experiments, each with strongly opposing views of the case. In reflecting on these observations, we realized that they coincided with our personal experiences in committees, work groups, and review boards. Thus, a number of interesting phenomena appear, from observation, to arise when groups deal with complex information. Unfortunately, the sparse literature provides few opportunities to contrast our intuitions with data from learning and remembering in or by groups.

General Issues

According to Steiner (1972), a group may be viewed in either of two very different ways.

1. It may be regarded as "a critical aspect of its members' environment . . . a social context that exerts powerful effects on its members' behavior and thoughts [p. 9]."
2. A group may also be regarded as "a unit in its own right . . . an amalgamation of interacting individuals who collectively generate outcomes that are different from those any single member might produce alone [p. 9]."

The present review will initially focus on the first of these perspectives. Historically, much of the early research on group memory centered on this topic. The productivity of individuals was studied under conditions of mere and inferred presence of others, when audiences were present, and when the subjects were coacting with others. When compared with the productivity of individuals who worked alone, such experiments allow us to study the effects of subtle social processes on individual learning and memory. Moreover, reflecting first on this simpler situation will enable us to develop some of the concepts necessary for the subsequent analysis of the more complex case of interpersonal interaction (Kelley & Thibaut, 1954).

The next topic will follow from the second of Steiner's perspectives; that is, the focus will be on groups of interacting individuals. Following Davis (1969), the effects of social interaction will be considered at two levels. First, individual performance will be compared with the group response produced by interaction. Included here will be research using both between-subjects designs, in which the performance of groups is contrasted with that of different individuals, and within-subjects designs, in which the performance of pregroup individuals is compared with their later group response. The second level of analysis will consider the individual responses of ex-members following group interaction, to be contrasted with either the group responses or with the responses of individuals who did not interact with others.

Following the sections surveying past experimental literature as well as some of our own recent research on remembering in groups, the results of this review will be summarized in terms of potential implications for organizational effectiveness. The chapter will conclude with a discussion of research issues and likely trends from a group effectiveness perspective. However, before discussing the research on remembering in groups, it would first be useful to discuss exactly what is meant here by the term remembering.

What Is Group Remembering?

While the title of this chapter emphasizes group remembering, the discussion until now has focused on both learning and memory processes. These two terms may be best distinguished by considering the principle phases or stages of the memory process.

> Stage analysis denotes the separation of learning and memory processes into (1) acquisition—the placing of information into memory storage in the first place, (2) retention—the persistence of memory over passing time, and (3) retrieval—the extraction of information from memory storage when it is needed. Traditionally, the term "learning" has been assigned to experimental operations where primary focus is on the first of these stages and the term "memory" to the second and third stages [Crowder, 1976, p. 2].

This distinction between learning and memory will remain important throughout the chapter, especially when the conditions prevailing during information acquisition are compared with those existing while subjects perform a test of memory.

Measuring Learning and Remembering

Crowder has also delineated the role of memory in learning experiments.

> The change in the brain that constitutes learning corresponds to what gets entered into memory. However, this change, learning, cannot itself be observed directly and therefore some indirect performance test must be used to infer that learning has occurred. . . . To recapitulate and anticipate the present sense of stage analysis, therefore, the acquisition process (learning) must be studied only through performance in a memory test (retention plus retrieval) [p. 3].

The term "memory" therefore refers both to the product of the learning process and to the process of retention and retrieval of information. As a result, studies that would traditionally be found in reviews of group learning (for example, the learning of lists of words, nonsense syllables, and paired-associates) will be included in this chapter. However, less symbolic instances of learning (for example, maze and motor learning) will be excluded from consideration.

Within the memory literature, a subject's memory is typically measured by means of either a recall or a recognition test. Interestingly, *none* of the studies of group memory employed a recognition test. Certainly, this is one attractive focus for group memory research in the future. (Recognition performance, in conjunction with sophisticated techniques such as signal detection theory, provide a much greater sensitivity of measurement than is possible from the use of recall tests. Use of recognition tests would therefore be quite profitable to the researcher interested in group remembering.)

The Influence of Others on Individual Remembering

THE MERE PRESENCE OF OTHERS

Social psychologists have typically employed two paradigms when investigating the influence of others on individual performance—one studying the effects of a passive audience and the other investigating the effects of coacting individuals. Of the experiments falling within the scope of this review, however, none have considered the effects of coaction. On the other hand, the study of audience effects on learning and memory has been quite extensive. Most of this research explicitly addressed Zajonc's (1965) drive-theory formulation regarding the influence of *mere presence* of others on performance. This simple perspective is important to a consideration of the more complex questions of group interaction because the presence of others is necessarily one factor in all such interaction. Most of this research has been well reviewed by Geen and Gange (1977) and will not be discussed in detail here. Instead, we will summarize only the central findings that have implications for learning and remembering.

Zajonc's Drive-Theory Formulation. Until 1965, conceptual accounts of audience influence on individual performance were in a state of confusion. At that time, however, Zajonc published a now classic paper that resolved the apparent contradictions of the field. According to Zajonc, the mere presence of others had a motivating effect on an individual. Drawing from Hull–Spence learning theory, Zajonc proposed that others enhance the emission of dominant responses by increasing the individual's general level of drive or arousal. Within a learning or memory experiment, the presence of others therefore increases a subject's performance when the dominant response is correct and hinders performance when the dominant response is incorrect.

In a study of paired-associate learning, Cottrell, Rittle, and Wack (1967) found support for Zajonc's hypothesis. Subjects made fewer errors when others were present if the dominant response was correct. Unfortunately, since the researchers confounded the presence of others during acquisition with their presence during recall, it is not really possible to determine whether the presence of others is influencing remembering in this study. That is, others were present while material was presented to subjects as well as during the recall test. Thus, it is impossible to know whether the effects of others' presence occurred during learning or during remembering.

A number of studies, however, have considered the separate effects of an audience during acquisition (Burri, 1931; Deffenbacher, Platt, & Williams, 1974; Ganzer, 1968; Geen, 1971, 1973, 1974; Pessin, 1933) and during recall (Ganzer, 1968, Day 2 results; Geen, 1973; Pines, 1973). Two generalities can be drawn from this research. First, it appears that relative to a control condition, the presence of others during acquisition hinders immediate recall but results in improved recall after a delay. This improvement in performance over time holds whether or not an audience is present at time of recall. Second, the mere presence of an audience appears to have no influence on subject performance at the time of recall. This latter result may at first seem inconsistent with Zajonc's (1965) formulation. However, in each instance where recall performance in the presence of an audience was unconfounded by audience effects during acquisition, it was difficult to determine whether or not the material subjects were remembering was dominant. That is, no differentiation was made between well-learned and poorly learned material. Thus, Zajonc's formulation would not necessarily predict either improved or inhibited recall in these studies. For the moment, however, no formulation satisfactorily accounts for these two general sets of results (for an alternative view, see Geen & Gange, 1977).

DISTORTING INFLUENCES OF AUDIENCES

Research conducted within the mere presence paradigm concentrated on the influence of audiences on the amount of material correctly recalled by subjects. When errors were discussed, they merely represented a transformation of the number of correct responses (1 − the number of correct responses) without describing the types of errors subjects made. The influence of an audience on the types of errors or distortions made by subjects was first reported by Bartlett (1932), albeit in the form of observational data from uncontrolled studies.

In a number of more recent studies, the attitudes held by an audience have been found to influence strongly the material recalled by subjects (Higgins & Rholes, 1978; Manis, Cornell, & Moore, 1974; Schramm & Danielson, 1958; Zimmerman & Bauer, 1956). Two types of errors have generally been noted in these studies. Higgins and Rholes (1978) found that subjects distorted the information they recalled about another person so that their responses presented a description more consistent with the attitudes held toward that person by an attending audience. In contrast, both Zimmerman and Bauer (1956) and Schramm & Danielson (1958) found that subjects were more likely to delete material inconsistent with audience attitudes than material consistent with those attitudes. Higgins and Rholes (1978) found no influence of audience attitudes on the types of material deleted from the subjects' recall. Perhaps subtle differences exist in the types of stimulus material that affect the types of distortion that characterize the subject. Finally, Manis, Cornell, and Moore (1974) analyzed their subjects' recall protocols by means of ratings from blind judges. These ratings were more positive when the audience was in favor of the issue than when their attitudes were more negative. It is impossible to determine, however, whether this influence was the result of distortion or deletion of part of the original stimulus material.

Audiences, therefore, have thus exerted a considerable influence on the nature of target subjects' recall. The extent of such influence has also been shown to increase over time, whether the delay is merely a matter of a few minutes (Manis, Cornell, & Moore, 1974) or a full week (Zimmerman & Bauer, 1956). On the other hand, Higgins and Rholes (1978) did not find an increase in the distorting influence of an audience on subjects' recall over a period of two weeks. There is some evidence then, that as the presented stimuli became more distant in time, the relative impact of audience attitudes on recall increases. Interestingly, the increased impact after delay is identical to results we have recently found when investigating the role of subjects' *own* attitude on remembering (Sheppard, 1980).

This last conclusion suggests that, in contrast to the social facilitation effects, the distorting influence of audiences occurs at the time of recall. Manis, Cornell, and Moore (1974) present evidence that supports this contention. In their study, Manis et al. found that subjects were equally influenced by audience attitude, whether they were informed of that attitude before or after they were given the stimulus material. Thus, at least in this study, the influence of audience attitude could not have occurred during acquisition. It seems likely, however, that audiences could have directive influences on the subjects' initial acquisition and organization of information. Experimental research into constructive memory effects (see, for example, Dooling & Christiaansen, 1977) support this contention. However, the effects of such variables have not as yet been demonstrated empirically for audience variables.

Potentially more interesting than the apparent impact of an audience on remembering is an ancillary result of the Higgins and Rholes (1978) study. The subjects' own attitudes, when measured some time after they had presented their recall, also shifted in a direction that was more consistent with the audience to whom they had addressed their presentation. Thus, in summary, the presence of a biased audience at the time of recall appears to have three related influences.

1. Subjects distort their recall responses and/or omit information so that the material they do present is more consistent with the audience's view.
2. This distorted recall appears to influence the perception of an unbiased third party listening to the presentation.
3. As a result of their presentation, subjects' own impressions appear to be influenced.

The practical implications of these conclusions are rather striking. They suggest that the presentation of information to some committee, board, or council will tend to be distorted in the direction of the group's prior established position. Moreover, both the speaker and those listening to the presentation will come to believe the facts as they are given. Any group having a clear position on some issue could therefore consider inviting influential persons to make presentations to the group. As a result of making these presentations, shifts in their positions on the issue (as well as the positions of others listening to the speaker) might be expected. Support for one's cause could therefore be elicited in a seemingly innocent manner. Interestingly, this line of reasoning suggests a mechanism to explain the inconsistent voting patterns of certain politicians. Perhaps changes in their votes, occurring after talks with groups of lobbyists, result from legitimate changes in belief and not simple expediency, as some cynics might suggest.

At a more individual level, a group member wishing to influence information presented to his or her group could also make use of this sort of mechanism. This could be done by encouraging future speakers to give him or her a personal presentation or briefing prior to the presentation to the larger group. The later presentation might then be somewhat distorted in the direction of this member's views.

One must also be aware of these subtle influences if one is to prevent distortions. For example, prevention of such influences might be accomplished by dissuading speakers from giving talks to biased groups, by attending their talks to make the audience more diversified, or by encouraging talks to a variety of different groups. It must also be mentioned that it is the perceived position of the group, not its actual position, that influences individuals. Thus, fact-finding groups, interested in receiving unbiased accounts of information, must do all they can to ensure they are perceived as impartial. By following these recommendations, one might best ensure that information presented, both in the current situation and at some later time, remains as accurate as possible.

Before going on, some caution must be imparted. Given the limited quantity of research (replications, etc.) and the inconsistency across studies in terms of the nature of the errors subjects make when confronted by a biased audience, it is clear that considerable supplementary research will be required before the phenomena outlined previously will be fully understood. Those wishing to make use of any of the recommendations just outlined would do well to test the results in their own situation before forging ahead.

Explanations of the Distorting Influence of Audiences.   The most obvious explanation for the role of an audience in remembering regards the response set a subject is apt to be taking in these studies. Allport (1924) has shown that, in the presence of others, subjects tend to give more moderate judgments of weights and the pleasantness of odors, presumably to minimize the possibility of being extremely different from others. Knowledge about the attitudes of an audience may therefore dispose subjects to withhold a response when it is inconsistent with that attitude or to boldly present the response, even if uncertain, when it is consistent with the audience's attitude. As a result, the subject's recall will be distorted in the direction of that attitude.

Such attempts to secure the approval or avoid criticism from others has been called normative social influence by Deutsch and Gerard (1955). A second type of influence, informational social influence, is also likely to occur in group memory situations. For example, Allen and Bragg (1968) found that subjects, hearing the responses of coactors in the situation, increased their memory performance when they heard correct responses and had poorer performance when they heard incorrect responses. In this study, subjects apparently used the information provided by the others when formulating their own responses. In a memory task, the correctness of one's own responses is often not objectively verifiable. One is therefore forced to rely on others to provide information, both as an aid in formulating a response and in the validation of the correctness of one's own responses, so as to be able to modify future answers.

To this point, we have been discussing the influence of others on memory distortion. Such a focus results from the tendency of research on processes like informational and normative social influence to look at factors affecting the deletion or distortion of stimulus material. Nonetheless, the same processes also operate on the subjects' incorrect recollections. Indeed, since such incorrect memories are not likely to be held with as much confidence as correct ones, audience influences may have an even greater effect here. As a result, one should not conclude that the operation of audience influences *necessarily* hinders performance in groups; it is possible that incorrect responses are either wihheld or modified, resulting in a better or more nearly correct response. Therefore, in an absolute sense, subjects' recall may be equally accurate with or without an audience. However, since subjects will be distorting (deleting) material inconsistent with the audience's attitude, irrespective of its correctness, their presentation will be clearly imbalanced in terms of the amount of information given one side. Again, this is particularly important if it later influences either the subjects' own or some other party's impression (or memory) of the object being discussed.

A Case of Active Audience Influence. The potential importance of this last point is particularly well exemplified by a series of studies conducted by Sheppard and Vidmar (1980). In these simulations of the pretrial legal process, it was found that witnesses interviewed by attorneys who were high in Machiavellianism (cf. Christie & Gies, 1970) presented testimony significantly more favorable to the attorney's case than either noninterviewed witnesses or witnesses interviewed by non-Machiavellian attorneys. From observation of the interview process between Machiavellian attorneys and witnesses, it appears that such attorneys actively encourage this kind of biased response during their interview. For whatever reason, this biased version then appears to transfer to the actual testimony the witnesses presented at the mock trials. Moreover, the decisions of judges listening to the testimony of witnesses interviewed by high Machiavellian attorneys tended to favor that attorney's client. Thus, again it appears that the potentially more interesting effects of a biased audience come *after* subjects have recalled information in front of an audience. Perhaps Machiavellianism should be employed as a selection device for any occupation requiring social influence as a major component (i.e., lawyers, salespersons, etc.). On a more serious note, the study of techniques employed by high Machiavellians (as well as others effective at social influence) would supplement our knowledge of the social influence process.

The Effects of Social Interaction

The effects of social interaction on task performance may be considered at two levels (Davis, 1969), a distinction that will be used here to facilitate discussion of the group memory literature. The first is the nature of the group response resulting from interaction; the second is the individual responses of the group members following interaction.

INDIVIDUAL AND GROUP PERFORMANCE

One comparison that has characterized research on groups from the beginning is that between the individual and the group (Kelly and Thibaut, 1954). A number of different individual performances have been employed in these evaluations, however. Group products have been compared with the average member performance, the best member's performance, and with various other combinations of the individual members' products. The implications of an individual–group comparison will, of course, depend on the specific individual behavior chosen for study. As we shall see, the experimental results are also influenced by the nature of the comparison being made.

When the recall of groups is compared to that of individuals, groups are invariably found to recall a greater amount of stimulus material. These results are obtained regardless of whether individuals perform as a separate experimental group (Hoppe, 1962; Lorge & Solomon, 1962; Perlmutter, 1953; Perlmutter & de Montmollin, 1952; Ryack, 1965) or are required to recall the stimulus material both as individuals and subsequently as members of groups (Dashiell, 1935; Yuker, 1955). The consistency of these results is quite remarkable, especially when one realizes that the members of groups generally were presented the stimulus material in the presence of one another and were asked to recall it immediately, a condition which was shown in an earlier section to hinder individual performance.

More useful than simply knowing that groups perform better than individuals would be some appreciation of the degree to which this is true. One approach to investigating this question is to compare group performance to a series of performance baselines calculated using models that assume that groups combine their information in a certain manner. For example, it is possible to calculate how many items, from a stimulus list, a group should be able to recall assuming that the group will recall every item that at least one member recalled individually (Lorge & Solomon's Model A, 1955; Taylor, 1954; Thomas & Fink's Rational Model, 1961). The superiority of groups over individuals is thus presumed to be due to the greater likelihood of having an individual who is able to recall an item; in other words, greater resources are available to the group. We consider below efficient use of those resources. For a description of a number of potential models for this type of research, see Davis (1973; in press a, in press b).

In addition to providing baselines (normative theory) which may be used to assess how well groups perform relative to an idealized criterion, research of this type can also provide a clue to the nature of the processes that may be going on in a group as they try to remember information. The direct and magnitude of the baseline-data deviation may provide a useful guide to explanation and further research. Unfortunately, almost all of the research using this strategy to data has investigated only Lorge and Solomon's Model A. Two key process assumptions are made in this model:

1. If one or more members know the correct answer, they will tell the group.
2. The group will always recognize this response as being the correct answer.

Thus, the model has received the label "truth wins" (Davis, 1973; Steiner, 1966).

Research on the Truth Wins Model.   One comparison often made in the group recall literature is tangentially relevant to the validity of Lorge and Solomon's Model A and thus will be discussed here.[1] When group recall is compared with recall of the best individuals in those groups (Yuker, 1955) or with recall of the best individuals in separate "nominal" groups (Lorge & Solomon, 1962; Perlmutter & de Montmollin, 1952; Ryack, 1965), the groups are found to be, on the average, superior. Group recall of a list of items or of an entire story therefore must involve more than the acceptance of any one member's individual recall.

Research actually testing the validity of Model A has produced mixed results. Studies conducted by Perlmutter and de Montmollin (1952, using nonsense syllables as stimulus items), Hoppe (1962, nonsense syllables when serial position effects are taken into consideration), and Ryack (1965, nonsense syllables) all obtained data that were generally consistent with the model. On the other hand, both Lorge and Solomon (1962, words) and Morrissette, Crannell, and Switzer (1964, three-digit numbers) found that Model A overpredicted group recall. Furthermore, a number of researchers have found evidence that groups sometimes contain members whose individual recall is better than that of the group, again suggesting an overprediction of Model A (Dashiell, 1935, classroom incidents and eyewitness testimony; Perlmutter, 1953, story; Yuker, 1955, story). In summarizing these findings, it appears that when Model A predicts results that deviate from

---

[1] Viewed as a baseline or as normative theory predictions, Model A would not, of course, be expected to yield a valid or accurate account of group recall.

those obtained, it is due to an overprediction of group recall.[2] Moreover, this overprediction seems more apt to occur when the stimulus materials are more complex in nature.

A number of explanations exist that can explain the "short fall" of actual group performance to predictions based on Model A. Two explanations focus on the pooling process itself. As noted earlier, members of groups are generally given the stimulus material in the presence of one another and asked for an immediate recall, conditions that were shown to hinder individual performance. Members of these groups are therefore likely to have fewer items available for pooling than individuals who are working separately. Thus, when the responses are pooled (either by the group or by the experimenter's treatment of the individual data), group recall will be worse than that predicted by the application of Model A to the individual responses. A second explanation is given by Steiner (1972). Steiner suggests that Model A might be considered as defining a level of potential productivity for the group. Members of a group, however, will not always perform perfectly. Process losses will occur whenever some member fails to present all the items he can recall to the group. The existence of such process losses will lead Model A to overpredict group recall.

A third explanation focuses on the decision aspects of the model. Thomas and Fink (1961) have pointed out that Model A is "rational" in the sense that members will adopt a response when its correctness is persuasively demonstrated. While this may be feasible in a number of problem-solving situations, it is often difficult to verify the correctness of an item retrieved from memory. As a result, the "truth wins" social decision rule may not really apply to a group recall task. Groups are more likely to use some rule that is more functional in this type of situation. For example, they may take a majority vote (cf. Hays & Bush, 1954). Unfortunately, neither a majority process nor other rules for selecting among items recalled have been given attention in studies of group memory—despite the popularity of such an approach in research with problem-solving and decision-making tasks.

A Comparative Test of Several Models. We recently conducted a study that allowed the comparison of predictions from several models with data from groups given both a recognition and a recall test. In this study, mock jurors viewed a videotaped trial and after a duration of 20 minutes were asked to recall all of the information they could from the trial. Subsequently,

---

[2] Similar findings have been found in research using problem-solving tasks (Davis, 1973). In fact, problems that emphasize the (social) processing of information show even more clearly the overprediction of performance by the "truth wins" principle of Model A.

they completed a 30-item recognition test based on the trial. These memory tests were either taken as individuals or in groups of four people. As expected, groups outperformed individuals on both the recall and recognition measures in terms of the greater amount of correctly remembered information and in terms of the smaller number of intrusional errors made. More important for present purposes, however, are the results of the model testing process.

There are two findings of note. First, looking at the results obtained for the recall measure, it appears that a "truth-supported wins" model best fits the data. This model suggests that the group will recall an item if at least two members in the group remember the item. Clearly, it would be premature to draw firm conclusions on the basis of preliminary results from one study. The form of group process model that best fits the data could vary for a number of reasons (e.g., type of material being remembered). However, this result, combined with the relatively poor support received by the Lorge–Solomon model in previous research, does indicate that it would prove fruitful to expand our thinking regarding the type of group process underlying remembering.

Second, when looking at the results obtained for the recognition measure, it appears that the groups specifically avoided errors of omission. In other words, groups were more apt to claim that an item was presented at the trial than to claim an item was a distractor. This tendency holds for both items that were actually presented at the trial (i.e., true items) and distractors. We have not yet determined whether this finding is a result of the type of decision rule utilized by the groups in this study or an exaggeration of a less pronounced individual tendency. However, the result suggests that perhaps we should reconsider the strongly held belief that groups are especially good at catching errors. It may depend on the type of error.

Group Error Catching—A Counterexample.   Results of a second mock jury study (Sheppard, 1980) are even more troublesome from the perspective of group error catching. As we noted earlier, individual recall appears to be influenced by the presence of a biased audience. One must therefore wonder if similar processes occur within the members of a biased interacting group. If they do occur, this suggests one instance in which groups may not catch more errors than individuals. One portion of the Sheppard study addresses this question. Results of this study suggest that subjects' own attitudes influence the nature of their recall. More important for present purposes, however, four person groups consisting of three individuals holding similar attitudes and one person of neutral persuasion were typically found to have even more biased recall than the most biased individual member. It has not yet been possible to determine whether this increased bias at the group level is the result of a particular decision rule, normative influence, or some other factor. However, it does appear that placing persons in a group may not always result in a reduction in the number of errors during remembering. In any spot where there is a greater concern for errors of ommission, the grouping of individuals could lead to problems. This suggests that nominal group techniques such as the Delphi (in which there is no face-to-face interaction) may be superior for certain uses (i.e., academic conferences, mediation boards, fact-finding committees). For a similar discussion of the potential effects of a biased group at a much more abstract level, the interested reader should see Janis (1972).

INDIVIDUALS IN GROUPS

Evidence has been given suggesting that recall by groups is superior to that of individuals working alone, certainly in direct comparison. Whether the members of such groups improve their performance as a result of the group experience remains, however, an open question. A number of factors suggest that group members will display superior performance. As a result of both normative and informational social influence during group deliberation, members are apt to adopt the group response as their own. Furthermore, as Davis (1973) has pointed out, even if members do not change their opinions during the group discussion leading up to a decision, they may experience postdecisional dissonance and change later. By adopting the (superior) group responses as their own, group members are likely to exhibit an individual recall superior to those individuals who have always worked alone. On the other hand, there are plausible reasons why members might not maintain the group response. For example, when the normative sanctions of the group are removed, members may revert to their previous answers—especially if uncertainties about response correctness exist. Also, members may forget the various decisions made by the goup. If either of these influences are dominant enough, postdiscussion member recall may fall below that of individuals who have worked alone.

Several results are relevant to the considerations noted previously. Crannell, Switzer, and Morrissette (1965) found that the variance of individual responses is greater than that of group members. Also, Yuker (1955) found that the variance of individual responses decreases after they have participated in a group condition. These results suggest that group members are affected by, and may have indeed adopted, the group responses. Moreover, individuals who initially recall the details of a picture or a story alone, then participate in a group recall, are later found to have improved their individual recall (Bekhterev & de Lange, 1924; Yuker, 1955). Participation in the group therefore appears to facilitate member recall. Unfortunately, an alternative explanation exists for these results. In both studies, individuals were presented with the stimulus material while they were in the presence of other group members. The increase in recall might therefore be the result of an increase in time between stimulus presentation and recall, a prediction supported by results from the mere presence experiments cited earlier (e.g., Deffenbacher et al., 1974; Geen, 1971; Pessin, 1933). Before we can conclude that the participation in a group recall facilities the members' individual performance, these explanations will have to be separated.

SUMMARY AND IMPLICATIONS FOR GROUP EFFECTIVENESS
IN ORGANIZATIONS

There are four general conclusions that can be derived from this summary, each of which has some implications for the practitioner concerned with effective group functioning. Consider each in turn.

1. Beyond the first few minutes, memory for information acquired in the presence of others appears to be better than if received when a person is alone. Therefore, at least some meetings, classes, etc. may serve as good tools for disseminating information in order to conserve time, space, money, etc. that would have been expended in presenting the information to each person separately. In fact, it is generally assumed that the presence of others necessarily results in some information loss. The reduced individual effectiveness is tolerated because of the overall efficiency of giving information to many people at one time. However, results of our survey of the research literature suggest that while less information may be received or learned in a group, information that *is* received appears to be better retained—at least when acquired and remembered under the conditions represented by the rather limited number of studies now available.

2. The process of remembering information in front of an audience or group possessing a consistent opinion appears to bias the content of a person's recall errors in the direction of audience or group opinion. Moreover, it appears that the person's memory remains biased after contact with the audience is terminated. This distortion has been found to influence both the person's own opinion and that of some other previously neutral party who listens while he or she presents his or her biased recall. Implications of these findings for group action were mentioned previously. However, some caution is in order. The robustness, boundaries, and major contingencies associated with such effects have yet to be determined.

3. There exists a small amount of evidence suggesting that individual memory improves as the result of *active involvement* in a group discussion. Thus, as noted in the first point, the group may often be a reasonable setting not only for the acquisition of information, but also for the consolidation of

information. This suggests that specific types of group settings—those requiring the active participation or involvement of group members (for example, seminars, discussion groups, etc.)—may be especially appropriate for the dissemination of information. Not only will group members be more apt to acquire the information as mentioned previously, they will also be more apt to maintain this knowledge following the group experience. A similar point has been made by Lewin (1947). In a series of studies designed to influence the food-buying practices of housewives during World War II, Lewin found that group discussion had a greater influence on subsequent behavior than the presentation of relevant information by means of an interesting lecture. The research we have reviewed here suggests one factor that could have contributed to these results.

This transfer of learning from the group to the individual is somewhat inconsistent with the findings of Laughlin and his colleagues Laughlin & Adamopolous, in press; Laughlin & Sweeney, 1977) in studying problem solving in which the task emphasizes the processing of information rather than its retrieval. They found that the strategies used at the group level in a concept formation task are not typically adopted by the individuals when later working alone. Research investigating differences between these two research orientations could provide some clue as to how and when group interaction aids or inhibits individual cognitive performance.

4. Finally, in small groups of the size that are typically used in our own research (4–6 individuals per group), group remembering processes appear to be best described by a model somewhere between a truth-supported wins model, in which a correct item is recalled if at least two people remember it, and a majority rule process. However, even this highly approximate summary is an oversimplification. Predictive models that describe group remembering accurately under various important conditions have yet to be worked out. Research directed at these issues is especially important from a practical standpoint because of the usefulness of such models in the engineering of more efficient group performance. For a detailed discussion of this point, see Davis (1980b). In the meantime, however, we will take a very broad perspective and consider probable group performance consequences of several familiar social consensus models, given individual member recall trends discussed earlier.

GROUP PERFORMANCE CONSEQUENCES

It should be clear from the foregoing that we are suggesting a temporal order of events. One or more group members must first remember an item or items of information. This information must then be publicized through discussion. Following any further processing or organizing of the information, potential group responses are constructed, only one or a few of which are ultimately selected by consensus. We have been concerned here only with the early stages of the sequence: (a) remembering by one or more individuals in a social context; and (b) group acceptance of that information for discussion.

The effects obtained from the conjunction of these two processes are not altogether clear, as the empirical evidence reviewed earlier has shown. Therefore, we would now like to explore some implications of conjoining a variety of possible individual and group trends. For example, an increase in the number of companions (as audience and–or coworkers) may _decrease_ the probability of remembering by an individual (depending on conditions as detailed earlier); however, the increase in group size may still _increase_ the total resources available for recall. Of course, such grouping activities are not passive. Social process increments or losses exist, stemming from the publicization of individually remembered information, and may be summarized by some sort of consensus rule. What is the final outcome to be expected from the conjunction of these various processes? We explore several answers in the following two sections.

Individual Level Trends. We shall restrict our interest to the probability p_r with which an individual recalls a given item of information in a group of size r. The isolate therefore recalls with probability p_1, the member of a dyad with probability p_2, and so on. Most empirical investigations and models of group performance alike (see Davis, in press-b) have, at least implicitly, assumed that p_r is constant for all r, a highly suspect assumption in general, as we noted earlier. [Many _empirical_ studies contrasting individuals with groups have avoided dealing with this problem (i.e., posed by $p_r \neq p_{r+1}$) by assessing the remembering of the individuals when they were in noninteracting groups; thus, any audience or coaction effects were included in the individual estimates of remembering.] Unfortunately, since so few relevant data are available, the _form_ of the function relating p_r and r is highly conjectural. Moreover, it is apt to change under various conditions (for example, from an immediate remembering situation to one of greater delay).

Consequently, we will entertain here several plausible function forms. Our aim is to explore the widely possible implications of different kinds of input when acted on by some social consensus process that subsequently publicizes the remembered item. To this end, we posed the hypothetical trends displayed in Figure 3.1. Panel A depicts a constant value of p_r for all r, and Panel B gives examples of linear trends. However, it is the negatively accelerated curve of Panel C and the negatively decelerated curve of Panel D that we speculate to be the most plausible forms for the widest array of

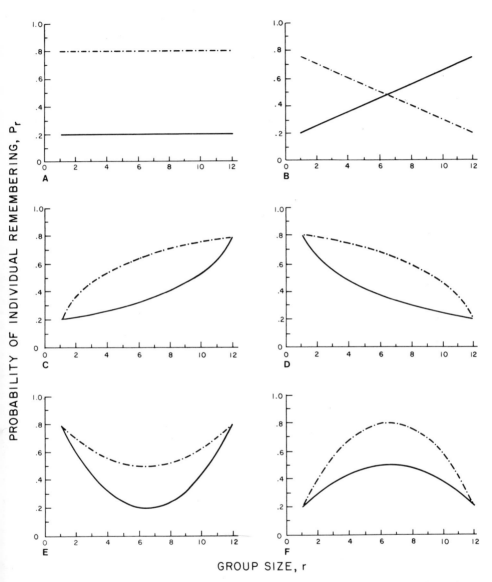

Figure 3.1 Hypothetical trends in the probability, p_r, an individual group member will recall an item of information with an increase in group size, r. Each panel displays two forms of the general trend.

59

situations. Even the nonmonotonic relationships described by Panels E and F cannot be ruled out for certain kinds of complex social contexts.

Group Level Consensus.   In contrast to individual remembering, an item recalled during group discussion may be misunderstood, rejected, or otherwise ignored unless somehow supported by a critical mass of others. The size and nature of this critical mass is itself an interesting empirical question, although likely to vary with material to be remembered, social context, and perhaps other variables as well. In particular, the social consensus rule *per se* may depend on, among other things, the number of discussants. Certainly, increasing group size increases the resources (information) available for pooling, although items can be missed due to increasingly difficult internal management (faulty social process according to Steiner, 1972). For example, observers of our mock jury experiments have noted informally that correct items of testimony arise during deliberation, but fail to be accepted or even remain actively discussed. It appears from observation that such facts are lost or discarded because they lack some critical level of support from the group.

Unfortunately, we have no clear empirical indication as to the most frequently occurring social support process for placing an "acceptably recalled" fact before the group. Consequently, we must again consider several social consensus rules for summarizing such processes. (While the ones chosen are intuitively appealing, they should not be considered as logically exhausting all possibilities.) Our aim is to pair the input displayed in Figure 3.1 with each of a small set of social consensus rules in order to study the consequences of the several conjunctions at each value of group size r. The social consensus rules for the "thought experiment" we are conducting (cf. Davis, 1980b) are given in Table 3.1 for six- and nine-person groups. As previously mentioned, the "truth wins" consensus rule operates on the principle that a group responds correctly if it contains at least one member who correctly recalls the item (see Davis, 1969; Steiner, 1972). "Truth-supported wins" asserts that the group recalls correctly if at least two members remember correctly, suggesting that a pair constitute a kind of critical mass of support. The familiar "simple majority," of course, asserts that a majority establishes the response, correct or incorrect, and that an even split between correct and incorrect recalling members has only an even chance of being correct. The "DEST" consensus rule is notable not only because the matrix does not display a tidy pattern of probabilities, but also because its development was guided by empirical data. Laughlin, Kerr, Davis, Halff, and Marciniak (1975) estimated the DEST matrix from four-person groups working at a vocabulary test, resembling in some sense the collective recall activities that are the subject of our interest here. Subsequently, an appropriately generalized version of the DEST rule predicted performance of separate sam-

TABLE 3.1

Examples of Social Consensus Rules (in Matrix Form, C) for Summarizing Group Level Social Support Processes[a]

Member distribution (Correct, incorrect)	Group response							
	Truth wins		Truth-supported wins		Simple majority		DEST	
	Correct	Incorrect	Correct	Incorrect	Correct	Incorrect	Correct	Incorrect
(6,0)	1.00	.00	1.00	.00	1.00	.00	1.00	.00
(5,1)	1.00	.00	1.00	.00	1.00	.00	1.00	.00
(4,2)	1.00	.00	1.00	.00	1.00	.00	1.00	.00
(3,3)	1.00	.00	1.00	.00	.50	.50	.78	.22
(2,4)	1.00	.00	1.00	.00	.00	1.00	.18	.82
(1,5)	1.00	.00	.00	1.00	.00	1.00	.00	1.00
(0,6)	.00	1.00	.00	1.00	.00	1.00	.18	.82
(9,0)	1.00	.00	1.00	.00	1.00	.00	1.00	.00
(8,1)	1.00	.00	1.00	.00	1.00	.00	1.00	.00
(7,2)	1.00	.00	1.00	.00	1.00	.00	1.00	.00
(6,3)	1.00	.00	1.00	.00	1.00	.00	1.00	.00
(5,4)	1.00	.00	1.00	.00	1.00	.00	1.00	.00
(4,5)	1.00	.00	1.00	.00	.00	1.00	.38	.62
(3,6)	1.00	.00	1.00	.00	.00	1.00	.28	.72
(2,7)	1.00	.00	1.00	.00	.00	1.00	.18	.82
(1,8)	1.00	.00	.00	1.00	.00	1.00	.00	1.00
(0,9)	.00	1.00	.00	1.00	.00	1.00	.18	.82

[a] The entries C_{ij} are the probabilities of the jth group response, given the ith distribution of member recall. Entries where C_{ij} = 1.00 or .00 should be considered approximations to true values that are very near but not in fact equal to 1.00 or .00.

ples of three- and five-person groups. (See Laughlin *et al.*, 1975, for a more detailed discussion.)

Exactly analogous to social decision scheme theory (see Davis, 1973; Stasser, Kerr, & Davis, 1980), which translates response preferences at the individual level into group-level decisions, the entries $[C_{ij}]$ should be regarded as conditional probabilities of the jth outcome (correct or incorrect) given the ith distinguishable distribution and (r_1, r_2) = (number of correct members, number of incorrect members) at the outset. For a fixed value of $r = r_1 + r_2$, and a given value of p_r, we may calculate the

$$\binom{2 + (1 - r)}{r} = m$$

probabilities, $(\pi_1, \pi_2, \ldots, \pi_m) = \pi$, corresponding to the m distinguishable distributions of correct and incorrect members, (r_1, r_2), from the binomial,

$$\pi_i = \binom{r}{r_1, r_2} p_r^{r_1}(1 - p_r)^{r_2}.$$

We may then calculate the probability of the group agreeing on a correct item, p_r, by noting that $\pi C = (p_r, 1 - p_r)$, where π is the m-tuple and C is the $m \times 2$ stochastic matrix with entires $[c_{ij}]$, both of which have been defined previously.

The examples of C presented in Table 3.1 represent social consensus rules that are well known from either custom or research. Thus, a "majority rule" may be specified by group constitution or bylaws, or emerge as an unplanned consequence of a group of individuals reaching some informal consensus. (See the discussion by Davis, 1980a, for apparent examples of the latter case.) "Truth wins" as a type of social process summary has often appealed to group problem-solving researchers (e.g., Lorge & Solomon, 1955) but has rarely been an accurate account of such data. (However, see the paper by Hoppe, 1962, and the discussion by Laughlin & Adamopoulos, in press.) Thus, we currently have few clear empirical guidelines as to when or whether truth wins, or how often any of the other social consensus processes of Table 3.1 satisfactorily predict group recall. The "truth-supported wins" and "majority rule" (for the acceptance of correct items and rejection of incorrect items, respectively) are something of an exception, as mentioned earlier. Still, the empirical support for these processes remains fairly thin. In any event, the sample of consensus rules in Table 3.1 spans a fairly plausible hypothesis space.

Each curve (trend) displayed in Figure 3.1, used as input, was acted on by each of the four social consensus rules described earlier and illustrated in Table 3.1. Results of these calculations are shown in Figures 3.2 through 3.7. Inspection reveals at once that group recall does not always parallel the trend in individual remembering with increases in group size, r. Figure 3.2 perhaps best shows the effects of social consensus rules, since p_r is constant—which we have observed to be a generally incorrect though fairly popular assumption. Most group changes with r are consistent with intuition, although the majority rule's dependence on the size of p_r (.20 in Panel A, and .80 in Panel B) is perhaps not in line with conventional wisdom. Counterintuitively, majorities in such situations exaggerate individual level tendencies; the low becomes lower and the high becomes higher.

Such a majority-exaggerating effect is perhaps even more evident for linear trends at the individual level (Figure 3.3); the group exceeds or falls below the individual level of recall, depending on the magnitude (i.e., size of

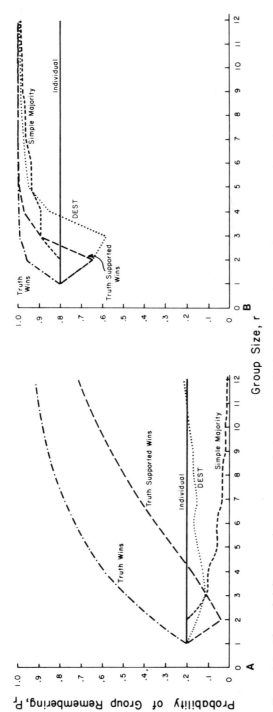

Figure 3.2. The probability, p ᵣ, of a group remembering an item of information as a function of group size, and social consensus rule (assuming individual recall functions of Figure 3.1, panel A).

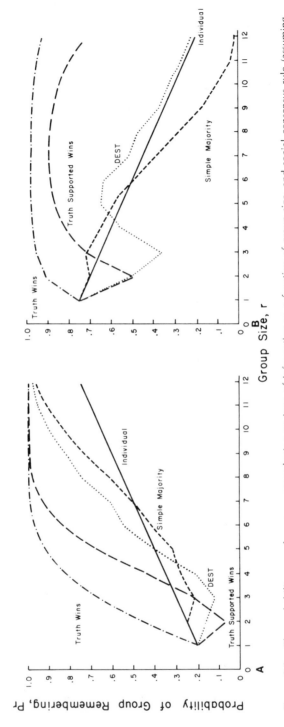

Figure 3.3. The probability, p_r, of a group remembering an item of information as a function of group size, and social consensus rule (assuming individual recall functions of Figure 3.1, panel B).

64

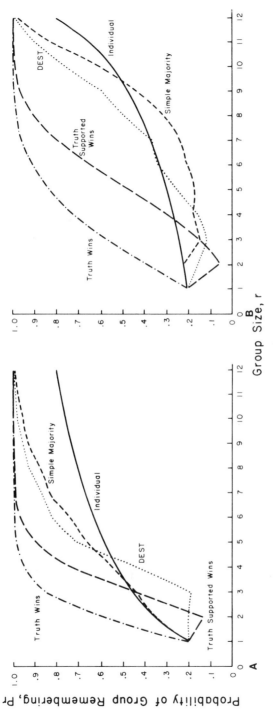

Figure 3.4. The probability, p_r, of a group remembering an item of information as a function of group size, and social consensus rule (assuming individual recall functions of Figure 3.1, panel C).

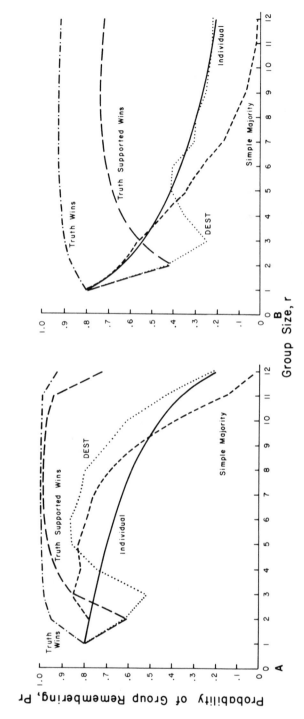

Figure 3.5. The probability, p_r, of a group remembering an item of information as a function of group size, and social consensus rule (assuming individual recall functions of Figure 3.1, panel D).

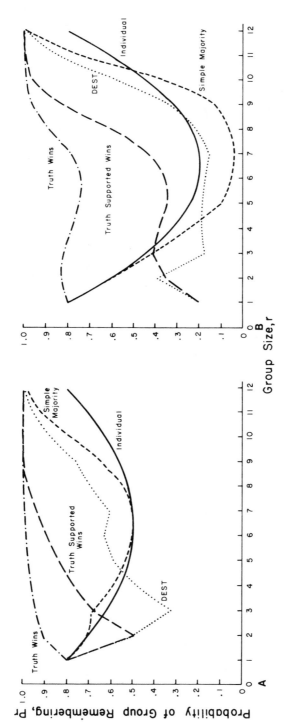

Figure 3.6. The probability, p_r, of a group remembering an item of information as a function of group size, and social consensus rule (assuming individual recall functions of Figure 3.1, panel E).

67

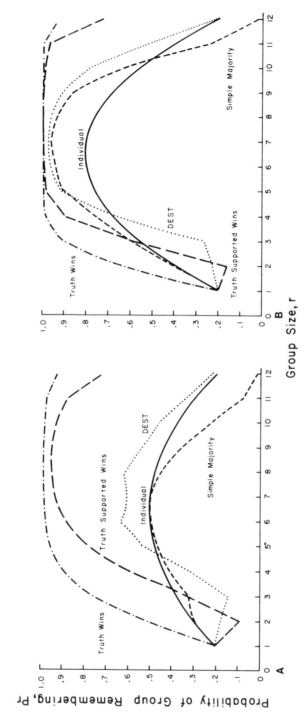

Figure 3.7. The probability, p_r, of a group remembering an item of information as a function of group size, and social consensus rule (assuming individual recall functions of Figure 3.1, panel F).

68

p_r) of individual recall. In other words, majority-inclined groups can actually supress information, which is consistent with anecdotes from mock jury studies reported earlier in that such groups generally reach majority decisions (cf. Davis, 1980a). Also, observe that the "truth wins" and the "truth-supported wins" rules have quite different implications for increasing and decreasing trends in individual recall. In particular, the trend of *decreasing* individual remembering with group size (e.g., Figure 3.3b), but with an *increase* in total resources (i.e., more members), produces interesting bowed curves at the level of group performance; such approach and retreat from an optimal group size implies necessary functional or practical boundaries to group size even when the group is operating on what is surely one of the most efficient social consensus rules conceivable in light of experience— "truth wins."

However, Figures 3.4 and 3.5 (especially Panels 3.4a and 3.5b) represent consequences of those individual recall trends we regard as fairly probable forms in light of our earlier discussion. The counterintuitive consequences of the majority consensus rule, and to a somewhat lesser extent that of the "truth wins" and the "truth-supported wins" rules, are again evident. However, it is the DEST rule that is most disorderly. Put succinctly, one simply does not expect the kind of nonmonotonic changes in these curves that are graphically evident. (Some lack of smoothness in all of these curves is attributable to rounding errors in what are discrete cases but which for convenience have been graphed as connected points.)

In cases where there is a *reduction* in individual recall with increasing group size, but an *increase* in total resources (more people to remember), it is difficult to assess informally or intuitively just what the outcome of this clash of forces might be. The empirical record is far too incomplete to be of much help. However, institutional needs for engineering an optimal work group size might require action before data could be gathered—even when such data are feasible. Thought experiments should prove useful for any group where consensus on information is required either as an outcome in itself or as an output for the making of decisions. Questions that may be addressed from this approach include those of optimal group size (i.e., what is the minimum-sized group required so that a given level of accuracy is likely to be attained?) and optimal group structure (i.e., what is the expected utility of imposing various decision rules on the group?). In order to be equipped to address such questions, a better understanding of factors influencing individual memory performance and social decision rules employed by groups in a memory context is needed. The sparse data on remembering in and by groups leads us to suspect such thought experiments will prove useful. Designed for extrapolating from existing data, or interpolating between data points, thought experiments are meant to be an aid to inference, organizational design, social engineering of groups, and so on—but not a substitute for data gathering.

Conclusion

Four general conclusions were derived from this discussion of the research in group remembering. The degree of fertility in this area is surprising, given the limited amount of research performed to date. However, the ultimate conclusion to be drawn from this review is that much remains to be done. First, each of the implications described in this chapter requires elaboration and testing in the field. Also, the general delineation of when groups aid or hinder learning and remembering requires greater concern. The impact of different remembering phenomena on other issues in group interaction and decision making should be investigated. Means for mapping individual memory results onto group remembering processes needed to be found (see Hastie, Penrod, and Pennington, in press, for discussion of this point). Finally, the relationship between information processing in groups and other social psychological phenomena (i.e., power, conformity, attitude formation, roles, etc.) deserves consideration. Given the utility of the research conducted to this point, the prognosis for further work on group remembering is extremely bright.

References

Allen, V. L., & Bragg, B. W. Effect of group pressure on memory. *Journal of Psychology*, 1968, 69, 19–32.

Allport, F. H. *Social psychology*. Boston: Houghton-Mifflin, 1924.

Bartlett, F. C. *Remembering*. Cambridge, England: Cambridge University Press, 1932.

Bekhterev, W., & de Lange, M. Die ergbnisse des experiments auf dem gebiete der kollectiven reflexologie. Reported in J. F. Dashiell, 1935.

Burri, C. The influence of an audience upon recall. *Journal of Educational Psychology*, 1931, 22, 683–690.

Cattell, R. B. On the theory of group learning. *Journal of Social Psychology*, 1953, 37, 27–52.

Christie, R., & Geis, F. L. (eds.) *Studies in Machiavellianism*. New York: Academic Press, 1970.

Cottrell, N. B., Rittle, R. H., & Wack, D. L. The presence of an audience and list type (competitional or noncompetitional) as joint determinants of performance in paired-associate learning. *Journal of Personality*, 1967, 35, 425–434.

Crannell, C. W., Switzer, S. A., & Morrissette, J. O. Individual performance in cooperative and independent groups. *Journal of General Psychology*, 1965, 73, 231–236.

Crowder, R. G. *Principles of learning and memory*. Hillsdale, New Jersey: Erlbaum, 1976.

Dashiell, J. F. Experimental studies of the influence of social situations on the behavior of individual human adults. In C. Murchison (Ed.), *Handbook of Social Psychology*. Worcester, Massachusetts: Clark University Press, 1935.

Davis, J. H. *Group performance*. Reading, Massachusetts: Addison-Wesley, 1969.

Davis, J. H. Group decision and social interaction: A theory of social decision schemes. *Psychological Review*, 1973, 80, 97–125.

Davis, J. H. Group decision and procedural justice. In M. Fishbein (Ed.), *Progress in social psychology.* Hillsdale, New Jersey: Erlbaum, 1980a.

Davis, J. H. The evaluation of existing and proposed social programs with minimal data: Examples from small group research. Paper presented at the Social Psychology and Social Policy Workshop, University of Kent, Canterbury, United Kingdom, 1980b.

Davis, J. H. Social interaction as a combinatorial process in group decision. In H. Brandstatter, J. H. Davis & G. Stocker-Kreichgauer (Eds.), *Group decision making.* London: Academic Press, in press. (a)

Davis, J. H. Group performance: Theories and concepts. In C. G. McClintock & J. Maki (Eds.), *Social psychological theory.* New York: Holt, Rinehart & Winston, in press. (b)

Davis, J. H., Laughlin, P. R., & Komorita, S. S. The social psychology of small groups: Cooperative and mixed-motive interaction. *Annual Review of Psychology,* 1976, *27,* 501–541.

Deffenbacher, K. A., Platt, G. J., & Williams, M. A. Differential recall as a function of socially induced arousal and retention interval. *Journal of Experimental Psychology,* 1974, *103,* 809–811.

Deutsch, M., & Gerard, H. B. A study of normative and informational social influences upon individual judgment. *Journal of Abnormal and Social Psychology,* 1955, *51,* 629–636.

Dooling, D. J., & Christiaansen, R. E. Episodic and semantic aspects of memory and prose. *Journal of Experimental Psychology: Human Learning and Memory,* 1977, *3,* 428–436.

Ganzer, V. J. The effects of audience presence and test anxiety on learning and retention in a serial learning situation. *Journal of Personality and Social Psychology,* 1968, *8,* 194–199.

Geen, R. G. Social facilitation of long-term recall. *Psychonomic Science,* 1971, *24,* 89–90.

Geen, R. G. Effects of being observed on short- and long-term recall. *Journal of Experimental Psychology,* 1973, *100,* 395–398.

Geen, R. G. Effects of evaluation apprehension on memory over intervals of varying length. *Journal of Experimental Psychology,* 1974, *102,* 908–910.

Geen, R. G., & Gange, J. J. Drive theory of social facilitation: Twelve years of theory and research. *Psychological Bulletin,* 1977, *84,* 1267–1288.

Hastie, R., Penrod, S., & Pennington, N. *Inside the jury.* Cambridge, Massachusetts: Harvard University Press, in press.

Hays, D. G., & Bush, R. R. A study of group action. *American Sociological Review,* 1954, *19,* 693–701.

Higgins, E. T., & Rholes, W. S. "Saying is believing:" Effects of message modification on memory and liking for the person described. *Journal of Experimental Social Psychology,* 1978, *14,* 363–378.

Hoppe, R. A. Memorizing by individuals and groups: A test of the pooling-of-ability model. *Journal of Abnormal and Social Psychology,* 1962, *65,* 64–67.

Janis, I. L. *Victims of groupthink.* Boston: Houghton-Mifflin, 1972.

Kelley, H. H., & Thibaut, J. W. Experimental studies of group problem solving and process. In G. Lindzey (Ed.), *Handbook of social psychology. Volume 2.* Reading, Massachusetts: Addison-Wesley, 1954.

Laughlin, P. R., & Adamopoulos, J. Social decision schemes on intellective tasks. In H. Brandstatter, J. H. Davis, & Stocker-Kreichgauer (Eds.), *Group decision making.* London: Academic Press, in press.

Laughlin, P. R., Kerr, N. L., Davis, J. H., Halff, H. M., & Marciniak, K. A. Group size, member ability, and social decision schemes on an intellective task. *Journal of Personality and Social Psychology,* 1975, *31,* 522–535.

Laughlin, P. L., & Sweeney, J. D. Individual-to-group and group-to-individual transfer in problem solving. *Journal of Experimental Psychology: Human Learning and Memory.* 1977, *3,* 246–254.

Lewin, K. Group decision and social change. In T. M. Newcomb and E. L. Hartley (Eds.), Readings in Social Psychology. New York: Holt, 1947.

Lorge, I., & Solomon, H. Two models of group behavior in the solution of eureka-type problems. Psychometrika, 1955, 20, 139–148.

Lorge, I., & Solomon, H. Group and individual behavior in free recall verbal learning. In J. H. Criswell, H. Solomon, & P. Sappes (Eds.), Mathematical methods in small group process. Stanford, California: Stanford University Press, 1962.

March, J., & Simon, H. Organizations. New York: Wiley, 1958.

Manis, M., Cornell, S. D., & Moore, J. C. Transmission of attitude-relevant information through a communication chain. Journal of Personality and Social Psychology, 1974, 30, 81–94.

Morrissette, J. O., Crannell, C. W., & Switzer, S. A. Group performance under various conditions of work load and information redundancy. Journal of General Psychology, 1964, 71, 337–347.

Perlmutter, H. V. Group memory of meaningful material. Journal of Psychology, 1953, 35, 361–370.

Perlmutter, H. V., & de Montmollin, G. Group learning of nonsence syllables. Journal of Abnormal and Social Psychology, 1952, 47, 762–769.

Pessin, J. The comparative effects of social and mechanical stimulation on memorizing. American Journal of Psychology, 1933, 45, 263–270.

Pines, H. A. An attributional analysis of locus of control orientation and source of informational dependence. Journal of Personality and Social Psychology, 1973, 26, 262–272.

Ryack, B. L. A comparison of individual and group learning of nonsense syllables. Journal of Personality and Social Psychology, 1965, 2, 296–299.

Schramm, W., & Danielson, W. Anticipated audiences as determinants of recall. Journal of Abnormal and Social Psychology, 1958, 56, 292–283.

Sheppard, B. H. Opinions and remembering revisited. Unpublished dissertation, University of Illinois, 1980.

Sheppard, B. H., & Vidmar, N. Adversary pretrial procedures and testimonial evidence: Effects of lawyer's role and Machiavellianism. Journal of Personality and Social Psychology, 1980, 39, 320–332.

Stasser, G., Kerr, N. L., & Davis, J. H. Influence processes in decision making: A modeling approach. In P. B. Paulus (Ed.), Psychology of Group Influence. Hillsdale, New Jersey: Erlbaum, 1980.

Steiner, I. D. Models for inferring relationships between group size and potential group productivity. Behavioral Science, 1966, 11, 273–283.

Steiner, I. D. Group Process and Productivity. New York: Academic Press, 1972.

Taylor, D. W. Problem solving by groups. Proceedings of the Fourteenth International Congress of Psychology, Montreal, June, 1954.

Thomas, E. J., & Fink, C. F. Models of group problem solving. Journal of Abnormal and Social Psychology, 1961, 63, 53–63.

Yuker, H. E. Group atmosphere and memory. Journal of Abnormal and Social Psychology, 1955, 51, 17–23.

Zajonc, R. B. Social facilitation. Science, 1965, 149, 269–274.

Zimmerman, C., & Bauer, R. A. The effect of an audience upon what is remembered. Public Opinion Quarterly, 1956, 20, 238–248.

4

Game Theory and the Structure of Decision-Making Groups

J. KEITH MURNIGHAN

EDITOR'S INTRODUCTION

A view of group decision making from a game theory perspective is provided by J. Keith Murnighan in this chapter. This perspective adopts some strong assumptions about the behavior of group members not made by other perspectives, such as that of rational action by decision-making group members toward the end of maximizing individual outcomes from decision making. While the veracity of such assumptions is questionable, Murnighan points out that they provide means for organizing an understanding of behavior in decision-making groups.

At first, these assumptions may suggest a strong likelihood of competitive behavior among members within a decision-making group as each strives to achieve their own gains and benefits. Group decision making, however, is often of a cooperative rather than competitive nature. That is, it is possible for individual group members to attain their own gains in ways that do not preclude the attainment of gains of others. It is situations such as these to which this chapter is directed.

Murnighan's game theoretic view is much concerned with the effects of power difference among members of decision-making groups and the impact of those differences. This concern is a vital one, for decision-making groups in organizations are often marked by status or power differences among mem-

73

bers drawn from different organizational positions. Much of the research relevant to the effect of power differences on decision making concerns the formation of coalitions within groups as means of controlling or gaining power. Murnighan considers this research, and goes on to consider evidence pertaining to the interplay of decision rules and power differences and its effects on group decision making. Also, he shows that a game theoretic perspective suggests a number of ways of improving the performance of decision-making groups.

The effects of group structure on the interactions of group members has been a central concern of researchers and theorists even before the heyday of research on group dynamics in the 1950s (e.g., Cartwright & Zander, 1968; Lewin, Lippitt, & White, 1939; Sherif, 1936). The primary empirical approach to the structure of groups has been to investigate patterns, norms, and roles that differentiate individuals on the basis of friendship, communication, power, status, and leadership. Clearly, these factors overlap with one another. In addition, rather than being treated in formal, precise ways (e.g., graph theory), they are typically discussed informally and intuitively. For instance, the structure of a group where everyone can and does communicate with everyone else is said to differ from a structure where communication is limited in particular ways. The difficulty with this and other informal descriptions of group structure is their inability to deal parsimoniously with the multitude of different group structures that can arise, and to deal with them in a coherent fashion. This paper uses game theory to analyze a wide variety of group structures by focusing on the distribution of power among group members. This power distribution influences both people's behavior and the consequences of their actions. A strength of the game theoretic approach is that it treats interpersonal power in a formal way, making the use of ambiguous descriptive labels unnecessary in the study of group structure.

In addition to a direct use of game theory as an analytical tool, this chapter will summarize a selected body of relevant research with a focus on application to intact, functioning groups. Thus, the bridges between formal theory, empirical research, and direct application will all be addressed.

Game Theory

Game theory has been the dominant theoretical framework used by economists and mathematicians to analyze the intricacies of situations (games) involving conflicting preferences among individuals (players). Rapoport (1960) has differentiated between games and other conflict situations such as fights or debates: In a fight you attempt to hurt your opponent; in a debate you try to persuade your opponent; and in a game you attempt to outwit your opponent. Thus, in viewing decision-making groups from a game theoretic perspective, the focus is on strategy formulation and implementation. An underlying assumption concerning individuals in groups, then, is that they will act strategically.

As with most economic models, game theory makes several strong assumptions. Basic to the assumption of strategic action are two others. First is the assumption of rational play: Individuals are assumed to attempt to maximize their utilities in any game. And, second, most game theoretic models assume that the players have complete information about the strategies available to them and to their opponents. The maximizing assumption simplifies much of the theory, but reduces its applicability to real world groups and complicates measurement problems. These limitations must be kept in mind as one discusses the game theoretic approach to group structure. Nevertheless, because a maximizing model can be forcefully utilized in explaining much of human behavior, game theory can serve well as a heuristic, analytical device in many settings. This point will be emphasized again later. The assumption of complete information reduces game theory's analysis to the effects of the game and its rules, ignoring the differences between the players (except those that are game-determined). Personal characteristics (which may be hidden from view and therefore not part of the information available to all) and the interaction of the personal characteristics of the group's members are not considered within the realm of game theory. All of the players are assumed to know the game and all of its intricacies, and to be able to choose among a multitude of possible strategies so as to maximize their outcomes. From a psychological point of view, the game theoretic approach stresses the situation over the individual, much like current day social psychological theory.

Decision-Making Groups

In applying game theory to decision-making groups, the first question is one of defining the situation and, thus, the game. In its simplest description, the game of group decision making consists of a set of individuals, each of whom holds a set of preferences for a set of possible decisions, and a decision process that determines how those preferences will be combined to yield a decision. The decision, in turn, may result in particular outcomes that may distribute benefits (or costs) to each of the group members. Because communication is possible and binding agreements can be made, group decision making qualifies as a game that is *cooperative*. This merely means that an individual can concentrate on obtaining benefits, without concentrating solely on self-preservation and protection (which is the case in noncooperative games).

The problem of finding some decision-making process that will equitably represent the preferences of all of the individuals involved has intrigued theorists for over two hundred years. In the 1700s, Borda and Condorcet both proposed procedures that would yield clear decisions in most cases. Condorcet's criterion for a group decision was reached if a single alternative won over half of the votes of the group members when it was paired against every other alternative. A series of votes were taken, then, between pairs of alternatives until Condorcet's criterion was reached. Borda, on the other hand, asked the group members to rank all of the alternatives. If there were n alternatives, Borda awarded $(n - 1)$ points to each alternative that received a first-place vote, $(n - 2)$ points for each second-place vote, etc. The points were totalled and the alternative that received the most points (and therefore held the highest average ranking of the alternatives) was chosen.

Borda and Condorcet's procedures did not always yield a unique decision, and the decision that was reached was in some cases obviously inequitable. In the 1800s, C. L. Dodgson (whose pseudonym is much more familiar—he wrote *Alice in Wonderland* and *Through a Glass Darkly* as Lewis Carroll) wrote several papers concerning the problems of majority rule, concluding that, for some set of preferences, any majority decision process will be inequitable some of the time (see Black, 1958, for Dodgson's papers). Dodgson suggested another decision procedure that first used Condorcet's criterion, but added a concept that might be called the "small change principle" when the Condorcet criterion yielded no winner: Dodgson's method asked the individual whose preferences would require the least change to do so if the change would result in a group decision that gave no advantage to the status quo (which is the usual case). It was not until Kenneth Arrow (1951) showed that, given some fairly weak assumptions about an individual's preferences and the decision procedure (any preference ordering is allowed; no one should be a dictator; the group's preference for *a* over *b* should not change when *c* is introduced, etc.), no decision process is generally equitable. Although many authors have weakened Arrow's assumptions in attempts to find a generally applicable decision process, most conclude by stating the boundary conditions for a particular process. The collected wisdom of these papers might be put into practice by choosing different decision procedures for different situations. However, the possibility that someone will misrepresent his preferences to obtain a decision process that increases the chances of having his most preferred alternative chosen as the group's decision is unavoidable.

Group Decision Processes

Although each group decision process will be inequitable for some group members in some situations, groups do make decisions. We must turn, then, to an examination of the different decision processes that groups do use. Fortunately, although their formal rules make them very different from one another, in practice they may be quite similar. Thus, the informal processes used by groups may not vary much, allowing for simpler and more pointed analyses.

In this discussion, we assume that the problem in need of a solution, or the issue in need of a decision, has been identified. Also taken as given is an early stage in the problem-solving process: the generation of viable alternatives. A final restriction is made—we are only considering here decisions that are not in any sense "correct." Judgmental, opinion-based decisions are the domain of this discussion.[1] (And, indeed, this is one way of differentiating between problem solving and decision making.) Although facts and information may be brought to bear in a discussion, how those facts and information are to be used will be assumed to be open to question.

Typical group decision processes include unanimity, consensus, several forms of majority rule, and hierarchical decision processes that differentiate among the members as to the impact of their preferences in determining the decision.

1. *Unanimity* simply means that all must agree; if a vote is taken, any group member can veto a proposal by voting against it. The unanimous decision process does not specify how a group decides among alternatives; it merely indicates that all must agree with at least one alternative.

2. The *consensus* process is similar, with the addition of the notion that compromise is appropriate. Again, all group members must agree with the final solution, but with consensus there is usually at least an implicit norm that the group should seek a solution that satisfies everyone. This differs somewhat from the notion of unanimity, which assumes that everyone will obtain their optimal outcome (or very close to it).

3. *Majority rule* can take many forms (see Dodgson's papers for examples). For instance, individuals can all vote for their most preferred alterna-

---

[1] These restrictions limit the generalizability of our results, albeit to what appear to be very interesting issues. Nevertheless, it is important to note that the identification of the problem, the generation of the alternatives, and the presence of problems that are amenable to optimization or other procedures are also important and worthy of considerable research. They do not, however, lend themselves to a discussion based on the philosophy of game theory and, therefore, are left to other papers.

tive, and the alternative receiving the most votes wins. Should the winning alternative not receive at least half of the votes cast, the process is termed plurality; with over half of the votes, the process is one of absolute majority. Other common forms of majority rule include voting on pairs of alternatives, with the winner in each pairing included in the subsequent pairing: The last remaining alternative is chosen. Roberts' Rules of Order follows this format. Should the winning alternative beat *all* other alternatives when paired with each of them, the process satisfies Condorcet's criterion for selection. The difficulties with Roberts' Rules of Order become important when an alternative is chosen that does not satisfy Condorcet's criterion because it was not paired against all of the other alternatives. A third variant of majority rule asks each voter to rank order the alternatives in line with their preferences; the group choice is determined by differentially weighting each voter's first, second, third, etc., choices, adding up the weights, and choosing the alternative with the largest sum. A procedure of this type is the Borda count.

4. *Hierarchical* decision procedures can also take many forms. Most typical of them involves a discussion of the alternatives by group members, with a single individual (the executive, the dictator, etc.) being responsible for the group's final decision. At the extreme of no participation is another example of a hierarchical decision process: dictatorship. Here there is no consultation; one group member (the dictator) simply makes the decision for the group.

Each of these decision rules has been investigated empirically, although the literature is not extensive. The work of James Davis and his colleagues (summarized in Davis, 1980a, 1980b) has systematically studied unanimity and a two-thirds majority rule process in the context of mock jury decisions. Castore and Murnighan (1978) and Murnighan (1974) studied the effects of all four types of decision procedures on the actual decision process and on the effectiveness of group members in implementing their group decision. The two sets of research studies consist of hundreds of groups, ranging in size from 5 to 12 people, facing different tasks, and using different forms of the decision processes. Thus it is extraordinary that they all tend to find, regardless of the decision procedure assigned to the groups, that a majority rule process does an extremely good job of predicting the group's decision. In both the unanimity and two-thirds majority groups in Davis' juries, whether they were 6- or 12-person groups, the process that best modeled the shift from individual preferences to the group's decision was a two-thirds majority rule process. (It should be noted that there are several two-thirds majority processes and that the different forms showed varying success in representing the actual process.) In Castore and Murnighan and Murnighan's groups, whether the decision process was unanimity, a Condorcet-like pairing of alternatives to reach majority rule, consensus, or dictatorship, a simple majority rule model was highly predictive of the group's decisions. This was true even in the dictatorship groups, where one individual was told that the group decision was completely up to him. Only a few people assigned to this executive position made full use of it; most took care to incorporate the opinions of the group members in the group decision. Thus, they acted as benevolent dictators. (The dictators whose groups made majority-like decisions also showed by far the greatest individual preference change following the group decision—allowing the majority to rule was highly related to them adopting the group's preference as their own.)

Thus, the evidence from experiments on decision-making groups suggests the potency of majority rule processes. This might suggest that our analysis should focus first on majority rule, later turning to other procedures. Unfortunately, the studies of Davis, Castore, and Murnighan have limited generalizability. All of their subjects were undergraduate students who had no previous history of interacting with one another in groups and who came to the experiment as equals. Unlike many real world groups that have established histories and clear status differences among the group's members, these studies were restricted to equals. That their decision procedure regressed to an "everyone's vote counts" majority process may not be too surprising. Research by Emerson (1964) and suggestions by Stryker (1972) support just this notion. Keeping in mind the consistency of the findings and their implication of the predominance of majority rule, it is important also to consider situations that vary the status or power of the positions held by group members. The dominant line of experimental inquiry in this area currently concerns coalition behavior. This literature can address the question of whether the presence of structure in decision-making groups (i.e., where status or power vary) affects the group's processes and the individual group members outcomes.

Research on Coalition Behavior

Our intent is not to extensively review the literature on coalition behavior. Interested readers can consult Chertkoff (1970) and Stryker (1972) for reviews of three-person games, and Murnighan (1978a) for reviews of some three-person, but mostly four-person and larger, games. Rather, the focus is on those experiments that considered several games, thus potentially revealing how the structures differed.

There are numerous models of the coalition formation process (Murnighan, 1978a); most attempt to predict that certain coalitions will form and–or that coalition members will receive particular outcomes from the coalition process. Most empirical studies of coalition behavior have been designed to test these predictions. Another way of looking at these models, especially when they make different predictions for different games, is to consider the predictions as indicative of different group structures. These considerations are particularly appropriate when a model predicts an overall outcome for each of the players. Take, for instance, the Shapley value (Shapley, 1953), recently reformulated by Roth (1977a, 1977b). The Roth–Shapley model determines the overall payoff (utility, gain, outcome) a player can expect from a game on the basis of his pivotal power, which is defined as the ability to change a losing coalition into a winning coalition. When all possible permutations of the players are considered (assuming players join coalitions one at a time), and the marginal value added to each coalition's outcome is attributed to the pivotal player, the Roth–Shapley value generates a unique group hierarchy on the basis of expected outcomes prior to the play of the game. Thus, in a three-person game where one player must be included in all of the agreements, and at least one of the two other players must be included in a winning coalition, the single, powerful player is predicted to obtain two-thirds of the total payoff, and the other players are predicted to average one-sixth each. This structure can be compared with other three-person` games. For instance, when any two of three players can form a winning coalition (an all-equal game), the Roth–Shapley value leads to expectations of equal outcomes for the three players (as do almost all other models). These two games, we suggest, have considerably different structures, and the group interactions that result should also be markedly different. Before turning to the use of a game theoretic structural framework in decision-making groups, we review the literature pertaining to group structure in coalition situations to ascertain whether the structure predicted to occur by the models actually develops in the interactions observed in experimental studies.

The first study to examine different games, and, indeed, the first experimental study of coalition behavior, was reported by Vinacke and Arkoff (1957). They studied six three-person games, varying the relationship among the resources (votes) assigned to each of the three players. A majority of the votes could be pooled to allow the coalition members to receive a fixed payoff. (When no coalition formed, the highest resource player obtained the entire prize.) The distributions of resources Vinacke and Arkoff studied included: 2(1−1−1), 4(3−2−2), 3(2−2−1), 5(4−3−2), 3(3−1−1), and 4(4−2−1). The number outside the parentheses indicates how many votes must be pooled for a coalition to win (for a decision to be reached). The numbers inside the parentheses refer to the votes held by the three players in the game. As they discussed the games, and as game theory would view them, Vinacke and Arkoff studied two different structures: all-equal and dictatorship. Even though the distribution of resources differed in the first four games, all have the quality that any two individuals can form a coalition that has a majority of the votes. The last two games allow the player with the most resources to win without reaching an agreement with any of the other players. Coalitions are not necessary here, and they do not threaten the individual who holds the most resources.

Vinacke and Arkoff's results indicated that structure was particularly important in determining the distributions of coalitions formed and the payoff divisions within those coalitions. The all-equal games led to the formation of a variety of coalitions, with those having the lowest number of pooled resources being most frequent [e.g., in 5(4−3−2), the 3−2 coalition formed most]. The dictatorship games were characterized by the nonoccurrence of coalitions: Since one player could win without forming a coalition, coalitions rarely formed. The payoff divisions generally gave more to those with more resources, particularly when the dictators formed coalitions (again, this was infrequent). In the all-equal games, any departures from 50−50 payoff divisions were minimal (even if in the 3−2 coalition, for instance, the player with 3 votes received only a slightly larger split of the payoffs than the player with 2 votes).

Vinacke and Arkoff's finding that those with fewer resources in the all-equal games were the most frequent coalition members was taken as a nonintuitive finding, since dubbed "strength is weakness." A follow-up study by Kelley and Arrowood (1960) showed that this effect eroded as the players continued to interact. The important point here is that the differences among the all-equal games was not as great as the difference in outcomes between the all-equal and the dictatorship games. Thus, without ignoring the effects of different resources, the effects of group structure on the bargaining process and outcomes of a game begin to be apparent.

As we have argued before (Murnighan, 1978a), three-person coalition games are limited to three underlying structures: the two studied by Vinacke and Arkoff, and a third, the veto game. (This assumes, of course, that a coalition of players can win—that all are not necessary to obtain a valued outcome.) In veto games, one player (the veto player) must be included in every agreement. In representing the three structures in three-person games as simply as possible, with the weakest of the players receiving a resource position of one and the other players receiving resource positions with the smallest possible number, we can depict the all-equal game as 2(1−1−1), the veto as 3(2−1−1), and the dictatorship game as 3(3−1−1). The only study known to the author to date to study the three-person veto game (Murnighan and Roth, 1977) did not compare it with the all-equal and dictatorship games. However, comparisons to the Vinacke and Arkoff study suggest that the veto players' payoffs were consistently greater than 50−50, which is the average for the all-equal players, and less than 100%, which the dictators approached. Thus, the structure of three-person groups appears easily discernible when the players' outcomes are considered.

Moving to four-person games increases the number of different group structures possible. In addition to analogs to the all-equal game [now a $3(1-1-1-1)$ game], the veto game [now $4(3-1-1-1)$], and the dictatorship game [now $4(4-1-1-1)$], there is a new type of structure called the apex game, modeled by this distribution: $3(2-1-1-1)$. In the apex game, the apex player, who holds two resources, can form a two-person coalition with any of the other players, and can only be excluded from the winning coalition by an agreement of all three of the nonapex players. Thus, where a unanimous revolt (i.e., a $1-1-1$ coalition) is only blocking[2] in the veto game and ineffective in the dictatorship game, it is *winning* in the apex game. Most indices of power would rank the dictator, the veto player, the apex player, the all-equal players, the nonapex players, the nonveto players, and the nondictators in descending order. Two additional veto games also become possible: $5(3-2-1-1)$ and $5(3-1-1-1)$. Unlike the analog to the original veto game, these two games require the veto player to form coalitions with two nonveto players in order to win in the $5(3-1-1-1)$ game, or one "privileged" nonveto player or the other two "nonprivileged," nonveto players in the $5(3-2-1-1)$ games.

From a game theoretic point of view, an increase in group size leads to a variety of new group structures. Unfortunately, there has been very little research contrasting the different structures possible in four-person games. The early research of Willis (1962) and Shears (1967) each considered two four-person games that had different structures. One of the games studied by Willis, however, was inessential (i.e., one of the players was not able to change a losing coalition into a winning coalition, thus, he was not essential to the play of the game). Shears studied the four-person apex and veto games: Her results indicated differences between the games in the types of · coalitions formed and in the payoff divisions (although these differences were not submitted to statistical test). In a third study of four-person games, Murnighan, Komorita, and Szwajkowski (1977) studied three apex games that varied the resources assigned to the nonapex players. Their findings showed no differences between the games as far as coalition frequencies were concerned, and some differences among the nonapex players' payoffs, with those holding relatively more resources obtaining higher payoffs. Finally, Michener, Fleishman, and Vaske (1976) studied 16 games, with three unique

---

[2] A blocking coalition is one that cannot win by itself but, once it forms, the remaining players are also not sufficient to form a winning coalition. Thus, in the $4(3-1-1-1)$ veto game, the $1-1-1$ coalition cannot win (it does not have a total of four votes), but it can block the player with three votes from winning.

TABLE 4.1
The Structures of Five-Person Groups

Name	Structural depiction	Presence of blocking coalition
All-equal	3(1−1−1−1−1)	No
Duopoly	4(2−2−1−1−1)	No
Pyramid	5(3−2−2−1−1)	No
Apex	4(3−1−1−1−1)	No
Limited all-equal	4(1−1−1−1−1)	Yes
Limited duopoly	5(2−2−1−1−1)	Yes
Limited pyramid	6(3−2−2−1−1)	Yes
Limited apex	4(2−1−1−1−1)	Yes
Veto 1[a]	5(4−1−1−1−1)	Yes
Veto 2	6(4−2−1−1−1)	Yes
Veto 3	7(5−2−2−1−1)	Yes
Veto 4	6(4−1−1−1−1)	Yes
Veto 5	7(4−1−1−1−1)	Yes
Veto 6	7(4−2−1−1−1)	Yes
Veto 7	8(5−2−2−1−1)	Yes
Veto 8	9(5−2−2−1−1)	Yes
Dictatorship	5(5−1−1−1−1)	No

[a] None of the veto games have yet been given names in the literature.

underlying structures. The authors noted the sharp differences among game types, and observation of the data suggests clear differences due to structure.[3]

Moving to five-person games, we see additional increases in the number of possible underlying group structures. Table 4.1 lists many of the possibilities. In addition to depicting each of these structures, a column was added to the table to differentiate between structures that allow the possibility of blocking coalitions in addition to winning and losing coalitions. Most research on coalition behavior has focused on games that do not allow blocking coalitions (i.e., proper simple games). Thus, there tend to be few data on situations where factions within the group can take intractable stances that yield no possibility for a decision. Real world decision-making groups, however, clearly include this possibility, as do all of the veto games.

Of the games depicted in Table 4.1, eight of them have been studied in laboratory experiments. Murnighan (1978b) investigated the all-equal, duopoly, pyramid (named here for the first time), and apex games with

[3] Identifying the differences that result from different group structures is made more difficult because most studies did not focus on group structure. Nevertheless, even without statistical analyses, the findings show clear differences in outcomes and bargaining processes (when they are reported) when group structure varies.

groups of experienced players. The all-equal game lends itself to a structure that changes little with group size: Everyone in the group has similar opportunities to communicate or influence either the decision or the distribution of outcomes. That no one is favored within the group may be fairly unusual in society. The duopoly game establishes a simple hierarchy of the "haves," the players with two resources, at least one of whom must be included in each agreement, and the "have nots," who must try to separate the two "haves" to find a chance at sharing in the benefits. The pyramid game differentiates the hierarchy into three levels. The player at the top of the pyramid, who holds three votes, can deal with either of the second-rung players, who hold two votes, or the two lowest-rung players. Similarly, the second-rung players have the choices of dealing with those above or below them in the hierarchy. The plight of the lowest-rung players appears much worse than that of the "have nots" in the duopoly game; their opportunities are severely limited. Finally, the apex game, with five players, has a structure similar to that of the apex games with fewer players. The differences lie in the greater difficulties the nonapex players have in uniting and the simultaneously greater ease the apex player should have in locating a partner.

The results from the study showed marked differences between the games, and, although the players' outcomes differed considerably from the specific predictions of the Roth–Shapley value, the rank ordering of the outcomes of the players in the different positions in the different games followed the Roth–Shapley prescriptions very closely. In a study investigating the first four of the veto games, Murnighan and Szwajkowski (1980) found differences in the payoffs to the veto players in the different games, but the differences were much less pronounced than those in the nonveto games studied by Murnighan (1978b). Specifically, the veto player in each of these games obtained such high outcomes, even when blocking coalitions could obtain substantial rewards, that the differences between the games were relatively small. (They were statistically significant, however.)

Recently, we have been collecting data that conceptually replicate the design of these studies, but place the players in markedly different environments. In the earlier studies, and in most studies of coalition behavior, players' interactions are severely constrained. Meetings are not face-to-face, and communications are typically restricted to handwritten proposals. The exchange, acceptance, and rejection of proposals determines the agreements that are reached. Argument and threat have little opportunity to enter the negotiations.

In our current studies, groups meet face-to-face. Although they are not assigned resources, they are presented with games that are identical to the structures of the original resource-based games. Thus, our current studies included all-equal, duopoly, pyramid, and apex games, as well as the first four of the veto games. The experimental situation models actual decision-making groups much more than previous studies. For instance, when agreements are made, all players remain at the table, unlike previous face-to-face studies (primarily with triads) where agreeing players left the room to determine how they would divide the payoff. In our current studies, no players leave the room during the decision making; they all have an agenda before the session begins; and all offers are put "on the table." In this way, we hope to span some of the differences in procedures in coalition formation and group decision-making studies.

The most significant difference resulting from the two procedures appears to have been a considerable drop in the payoffs received by the veto players in the four veto games. In the original Murnighan and Szwajkowski (1979) study, the veto players' mean payoffs were just less than 90 of the possible 100 points in each agreement. Because the distributions were negatively skewed, the median payoff (a better measure of central tendency) was even higher, at 95%. In the face-to-face games, the veto players' payoffs tended to fall around 65%. (The data have not yet been completely analyzed.) The data for the nonveto games revealed a drop in payoffs only for the apex player; in the other games, the players' payoffs appear to be quite similar to those found in the Murnighan (1978b) non-face-to-face study.

A final study that spanned several group structures and group sizes was conducted by Vinacke (1971). His groups varied in size from three to nine, including all male and all female groups; structures included veto games, dictatorship games, all-equal games, apex games, and games whose structure changed with group size. The results support Vinacke's (1959) propositions that males and females react to coalition bargaining very differently, with males acting exploitatively and females accommodatively. Vinacke (1971) observed little difference across structures for the female players, with marked differences across structures for the male players. From a game theoretic point of view, where the players are assumed to maximize their outcomes, the males satisfied the underlying conditions of the game theoretic models, the females did not. Recent additional support for the presence of sex differences has been published by Komorita and Moore (1976). Thus, females may be paying attention to variables other than those defined strictly by the game. Not surprisingly, male subjects appear to view games in much the same manner as game theorists, who are predominantly male.

The conclusion that seems to fall from these studies, especially when they are compared to studies where the resources change but the structure of the game does not (e.g., Murnighan et al., 1977), is that the underlying structure of the game is the most important determinant of the outcome of the bargaining. This also seems to be true of a very recent study by Kravitz (1980). He investigated four different four-person games, assigning resources in one set of conditions and not assigning resources in the other. His preliminary results show no marked differences between the conditions. Thus, in a series of studies, the game theoretic approach to analyzing groups seems particularly useful. Not only does it give us a well-formulated, specific model that can be used to analyze a variety of group structures, but it also is fairly predictive of the outcomes and processes of coalition bargaining. With this justification, we now turn to applying game theory to decision-making groups, analyzing their structure, and drawing some preliminary conclusions from this analysis.

Game Theory and Group Decision Structures

When we return to the different decision processes that are most often used in groups, we can ask what group structure each process promotes. The majority rule procedures are consistent with the all-equal games that require the smallest majority possible (if pluralities are excluded). If a majority rule process requires more than a simple majority, as was the case in the two-thirds majorities required of Davis's juries, we merely change the quota of votes needed to reach an agreement. Thus, if a two-thirds majority is required of a five-person group, we have a limited all-equal game, $4(1-1-1-1-1)$, with the possibility of blocking coalitions. (In Davis's groups, the presence of a blocking coalition resulted in a hung jury.) As Davis (1980b) has pointed out, the size of the group and the majority decision rule they use can interact, making different rules identical, depending on the size of the group. Thus, for a five-person group, the two-thirds majority is identical to the four-fifths majority. Depending on the size of the group, there are a limited number of group structures that can result from the imposition of majority rule.

Unanimity is a game that was not really considered in our discussion of coalitions because the concept of coalition implicitly excludes the requirement of a coalition of the whole group. Nevertheless, to put the unanimous decision process in the same framework as the other decision processes, we can consider unanimity as establishing an all-equal game that requires the largest majority possible: $5(1-1-1-1-1)$. Any single individual can now be a blocking coalition. The fact that such decision procedures result in greater difficulty in reaching a decision, and longer decision times (Castore & Murnighan, 1978; Davis, Kerr, Atkin, Holt, & Meek, 1975) is not surprising.

As our earlier discussion of consensus suggested, its demands on a group place it somewhere between majority rule and unanimity. Depending on the amount of compromise that the group members are willing to tolerate, we can depict consensus somewhere between $3(1-1-1-1-1)$ and $5(1-1-$

1−1−1). The lack of a clearcut structural depiction arises because the typical guidelines for consensus are also not clearcut.

Dictatorship is the most unequal of games: 5(5−1−1−1−1). The research on this decision process is contradictory. Vinacke and Arkoff (1957) and Vinacke (1971) suggest that, at least for males, dictatorship games result in no coalitions forming and the dictator taking the entire payoff; Castore and Murnighan (1978), on the other hand, found that decision-making groups with assigned dictators acted much like majority rule groups. Future research into the multitude of possible factors that could lead to one result or the other would be very helpful in this area. Nevertheless, we might expect from a game theoretic analysis of decision-making groups that the distribution of outcomes in dictatorship groups will be more disproportionate than any other group structure.

This limited enumeration of group decision-making structures, all of which are determined by the decision rule to be used by a group, has left out a large number of potential decision-making structures that may not strictly conform to easily recognizable group procedures. For instance, many of the structures listed in Table 4.1 are not included among our most often used decision-making processes. None of the veto games are mentioned, and none of the games that require a majority of votes (or resources), but where votes are disproportionately distributed among the players, are mentioned either.

The veto games clearly fall between the nonveto games and the dictatorship game in the severity of distributions and processes one might expect to find. Analogs to veto games are decision-making groups that: (a) can end up in a deadlock; (b) have a strong leader or central figure who nevertheless needs at least some support from some members of the group; and (c) may or may not differentiate among the nonveto group members, thus resulting in one or another of the possible veto games. One common decision-making practice in organizations resembles a veto game: that of a manager consulting a group of subordinates about a problem, yet retaining the final decision-making authority (Tannenbaum & Schmidt, 1958). A salient example is the judicious use of a panel of advisors by the President of the United States. Results from veto games should have some application and offer some insights into a variety of organizational decision-making settings.

The majority games where votes are disproportionately distributed are particularly appropriate models for groups that include members who have status, expertise, legitimacy, or some other recognizable resource that will play a part in the decision-making process. For instance, the son of the chairman of the board may have considerably more influence in decision-making groups ostensibly composed of equals. Or, in other cases, the individual people turn to, but who can be overruled if sufficient support for opposing decisions is present, may hold a position like the apex player, the duopolist (if there are two central figures), or the player at the top of the pyramid in the pyramid game. And these only refer to five-person groups! Larger groups allow even greater differentiation among possible structures.

What is interesting about the differences between the veto games and the groups that use a form of majority rule is that they are easily recognized: People can discriminate between them quite well. They all hinge on the ability or inability of group members to agree that "We can (can't) do without his or her support." Because veto and majority–unequal distribution groups generally direct most of the discussion toward the veto, apex, or pyramid players, differentiation among the remaining group members becomes difficult. This is particularly true for actual group members, whose affective responses to the group's interactions may interfere with their ability to make such pointed observations. In particular, the power of a consensus or a majority rule decision is very strong (Castore & Murnighan, 1978; Harnett, 1967). The apex player and the pyramid player may not appear much different from one another from one day to the next. However, outside observers may be able to identify subtle differences in processes and outcomes, and, if outcomes are recorded, archival analyses of the group members' outcomes might offer considerable insights into a group's structure. Unfortunately, there seems to be nothing in the literature on this topic. Such archival analysis, of course, assumes that the structure of the group remains the same during the course of the observations, and this may not necessarily be the case (although considerable changes are often needed before one structure evolves into another structure).

For most real world coalitions diagnosis of even the presence of coalitions within decision-making groups is difficult. But even if we do not consider these seemingly overwhelming observational problems, the use of game theory as a tool for understanding the structure of decision-making groups can foster improved decision making.

Before going on to applications, a summary of the impact of a game's structure on the decision-making processes and outcomes of a group is in order. The underlying model we have been discussing is an unidirectional causal chain. The chain begins with the group's decision rule (if it has been formalized), which dictates the kind of game the group will be playing. Thus, majority rule games, veto games, or dictatorship games can be specified by the decision rule. Getting more particular, the specific game a group is playing determines the structure of the decision process. If the decision rule is majority rule, the game can be all-equal, apex, duopoly, or pyramid (if we are dealing with a five-person group). An accurate depiction of the game allows us to deal with one of these structures. When no decision rule is formally specified, the game that exists, and the structure that follows, is more difficult to identify, but is nevertheless present. Structure, in turn, leads to a particular group process. The all-equal game generates diffuse communication patterns—any of the group can talk to each other in pursuing a decision. The apex game, on the other hand, typically results in communication directed toward the apex player. This is also true of the pyramid game, although there are additional possibilities here. In the duopoly game, two patterns develop: The duopolists deal with each other to the exclusion of the other group members, or they compete with each other in attempts to sway two or more of the nonduopolists to their position. Finally, the process that results determines the outcomes of the interaction—which policy is adopted, who receives what portion of the benefits or costs that accrue, etc. The system we have outlined, then, looks like this:

DECISION RULE $\rightarrow$ GAME $\rightarrow$ STRUCTURE $\rightarrow$ PROCESS $\rightarrow$ OUTCOMES.

Because the chain is chronological, it has additional face validity. Feedback loops might be added from outcomes to structure because the type of majority rule game that is played, for instance, may depend on the accumulated benefits (e.g., resources) players obtain from previous decisions.

The imposition of the game and structure elements within this scheme give it a strong theoretical and empirical grounding. As far as we know, our current research is the first to span the procedural differences between research on coalition behavior and research on decision-making groups. As research endeavors continue, additional possibilities for application may also develop. At this point, however, we can suggest some applications that may have meaning for decision-making groups in action.

Applications

Because of the findings that most groups move to majority rule decision processes, we will concentrate on majority rule. Most of our discussion should apply, although possibly to a limited degree, to some aspects of the other decision processes.

First, a knowledge and understanding of a group's structure can go a long way toward reducing the perceived conflict that may result when outcomes are distributed unequally or where the decision process limits the impact of an individual's preferences. Equity models (e.g., Adams, 1965) predict that people's motivation to change the status quo will increase as the imbalance of their input–outcome ratio, relative to the input–outcome ratio of other group members, increases. Individuals who see other's inputs as greater than their own can more easily handle other's outcomes that are also greater than their own. Indeed, compensation that is proportional to one's resources is *expected*. Thus, if one can accurately assess the inputs each group member has in the structural sense, then a distribution of outcomes that gives the greatest benefits to an apex or pyramid or veto player, for instance, should be neither surprising nor aggravating. And the fine discriminations made by the game theoretic models may yield the most accurate expectations.

The push toward majority rule decision processes, regardless of the rule prescribed, also suggests that groups that do not have institutionalized procedures that insure either all-equal, veto, or dictator games, may move toward majority rule processes that become more and more like all-equal games. Indeed, it would not be surprising to find individuals such as those at the bottom of a pyramid game attempting to change the situation to resemble an apex or an all-equal game. Although an apex game gives the pyramid player a greater advantage in becoming an apex player, it also increases the power of the weak players' positions, particularly relative to the two middle players in the original pyramid. Thus, structural changes may be attempted in some nonobvious directions by informed players.

With the increasing number of potential structures that arise as group size increases, the number of small coalitions that can control decisions also increases. This in turn increases the possibility for large numbers of individuals being excluded from winning coalitions. For instance, even in a majority rule game, if two players have duopoly power, three of the five players can easily be excluded from decision making. As this number of potentially excluded individuals increases, considerable discontent with the process may be voiced. Game theory might suggest that groups be formed with few members, thus reducing the number of different structures that can occur, the potential number of excluded players, and also the total pool of information within the group. This problem might be reduced by careful composition of the group. From a psychological point of view, small groups are also functional. It is easier to exclude a single individual (the fringe person who is redefined as not being within the central core of a group) than more than one. [Research on conformity (e.g., Asch, 1955) also suggests that this excluded individual might change his or her position to align him- or herself with the group, even though his or her preferences differ from the group's.] People should know about group structure from a game theoretic viewpoint, and game theoretic and psychological wisdom suggests that groups be kept small. If this is not possible, one faces the dilemma of reducing the potential exclusion of members while, at the same time, avoiding the ill effects of unanimity (i.e., long decision times and group member dissatisfaction).

Aspects of game theory's investigations into two-person bargaining also may have an impact on *n*-person games (decision-making groups included).

Recently, Roth and Murnighan (1978), building on Taylor (1976) and Luce and Raiffa (1957), showed how the effects of continued interaction combine with an opponent's strategies and the structure of a game to determine occasions where cooperation is an equilibrium ("rational") strategy. While most bargaining research has investigated games that have known endpoints, Roth and Murnighan (1978) presented examples of how the probabilistic termination of a game in part determined the likelihood of mutual cooperation. From a decision-making point of view, then, it might be suggested that continued interaction among group members would facilitate both the nonexclusion of group members and the continued consideration of each group member's preferences in attempting to determine which decision is most representative of all the group members' preferences. That the social interaction necessary for mutual cooperation also can lead to group inefficiency is yet another dilemma, but one that may be more tractable, especially given a cooperative atmosphere.

Further conclusions that might be drawn from this research are that the payoffs that potentially accrue to individuals who cooperate are very important in determining levels of cooperation. In particular, as the environment offers any pair of individuals (and, hopefully, larger groups making decisions) higher payoffs for cooperation, people will cooperate more. Thus, as the environment becomes more munificent, cooperative rather than conflictful decision making might be anticipated. Unfortunately, the designers of group systems engaging in decision making often have little control over the environment's rewards, thus reducing the direct applicability of this point. Nevertheless, a particularly skillful designer may be able to influence the perceptions of group members to the point where increased benefits are expected to follow from cooperative, conscientious decision making. Patriotism is one example.

Molding individuals' perceptions (which we have given no directions for implementing but which seems somehow to be within the grasp of particularly competent administrators) suggests another, similarly ephemeral prescription. This one is simple: Increase the trust of group members for one another and they will be happier, more conscientious, more cooperative, and better decision makers. Possibly the benefits that sensitivity group leaders hope for could be instituted within the membership of decision-making groups. Whatever technique is utilized, the reduction of uncomfortable, suspicious feelings about one another, much like the prisoners' dilemma game's need for increased cooperation in the face of "rational" uncooperative responses, is needed to improve the relationships of group members and the decision making that results. Thus, the process losses (Steiner, 1972) that are often noted in observing group interactions may not be losses in the long run if they allow group members to generate sufficient harmony and respect so that they can engage with ease in ideational conflict (conflict over ideas and issues) and avoid the disfunctions of interpersonal conflict. And, indeed, with groups that get along well and progress through problems efficiently, there never seems to be even the possibility that interpersonal conflict will occur. Possibly the investigation of the early processes of groups that develop trust versus those that develop distrust might highlight why different groups develop or don't develop harmony. In any case, trust is essential for a small group, interacting over time, to perform effectively in a decision-making capacity. And a little bit of information about the structure of decision-making groups would not hurt either.

ACKNOWLEDGMENTS

I would like to gratefully acknowledge the inspiration and comments provided by Sam Komorita, Al Roth, Rick Guzzo, and Moe Stein.

References

Adams, J. S. Inequity in social exchange. *In* L. Berkowitz (Ed.), *Advances in experimental social psychology,* Volume 2. New York: Academic Press, 1965.
Arrow, K. *Social choice and individual values.* New Haven, Connecticut: Yale University Press, 1951.
Asch, S. E. Opinions and social pressure. *Scientific American,* 1955, *193,* 31–35.
Black, D. *Theory of committees and elections.* Cambridge: Cambridge University Press, 1958.
Cartwright, D., & Zander, A. *Group dynamics.* New York: Harper & Row, 1968.
Castore, C. H., & Murnighan, J. K. Determinants of support for group decisions. *Organizational Behavior and Human Performance,* 1978, *22,* 75–92.
Chertkoff, J. M. Sociopsychological theories and research on coalition formation. *In* S. Groennings, E. W. Kelley, & M. Leiserson (Eds.), *The study of coalition behavior.* New York: Holt, Rinehart, & Winston, 1970.
Davis, J. H. Group decision and procedural justice. *In* M. Fishbein (Ed.), *Progress in social psychology.* Hillsdale, New Jersey: Erlbaum Associates, 1980a.
Davis, J. H. Social interaction as a combinatorial process in group decision. *In* H. Brandstatter, J. H. Davis, & G. Stocker-Kreichgauer (Eds.), *Group decision processes.* London: Academic Press, 1980b.
Davis, J. H., Kerr, N. L., Atkin, R. S., Holt, R., & Meek, D. The decision processes of 6- and 12-person mock juries assigned unanimous and two-thirds majority rules. *Journal of Personality and Social Psychology,* 1975, *32,* 1–14.
Emerson, R. M. Power-dependence relations—two experiments. *Sociometry,* 1964, *27,* 382–398.
Harnett, D. L. A level of aspiration model for group decision making. *Journal of Personality and Social Psychology,* 1967, *5,* 58–66.
Kelley, H. H., & Arrowood, A. J. Coalitions in the triad: Critique and experiment. *Sociometry,* 1960, *23,* 231–244.

Komorita, S. S., & Moore, D. Theories and processes of coalition formation. *Journal of Personality and Social Psychology*, 1976, *33*, 371–381.

Kravitz, D. Effects of resources and alternatives on coalition formation. *Journal of Personality and Social Psychology*, 1981, *41*, 87–98.

Lewin, K., Lippitt, R., & White, R. K. Patterns of aggressive behavior in experimentally created "social climates." *Journal of Social Psychology*, 1939, *10*, 271–299.

Luce, R. D., & Raiffa, H. *Games and decisions.* New York: Wiley, 1957.

Michener, H. A., Fleishman, J. A., & Vaske, J. J. A test of the bargaining theory of coalition formation in four-person groups. *Journal of Personality and Social Psychology*, 1976, *34*, 1114–1126.

Murnighan, J. K. *Coalition formation in decision making groups.* Unpublished doctoral dissertation, Purdue University, 1974.

Murnighan, J. K. Models of coalition behavior: Game theoretic, social psychological, and political perspectives. *Psychological Bulletin*, 1978a, *85*, 1130–1153.

Murnighan, J. K. Strength and weakness in four coalition situations. *Behavioral Science*, 1978b, *23*, 195–208.

Murnighan, J. K., Komorita, S. S., & Szwajkowski, E. Theories of coalition formation and the effects of reference groups. *Journal of Experimental Social Psychology*, 1977, *13*, 166–181.

Murnighan, J. K., & Roth, A. E. The effects of communication and information availability in an experimental study of a three-person game. *Management Science*, 1977, *23*, 1336–1348.

Murnighan, J. K., & Szwajkowski, E. Coalition bargaining in four games that include a veto player. *Journal of Personality and Social Psychology*, 1980, *37*, 1933–1946.

Rapoport, A. *Fights, games and debates.* Ann Arbor, Michigan: Michigan University Press, 1960.

Roth, A. E. Bargaining ability, the utility of playing a game, and models of coalition formation. *Journal of Mathematical Psychology*, 1977a, *16*, 153–160.

Roth, A. E. The Shapley value as a von Neumann–Morgenstern utility. *Econometrica*, 1977b, *45*, 657–664.

Roth, A. E., & Murnighan, J. K. Equilibrium behavior and repeated play of the prisoner's dilemma. *Journal of Mathematical Psychology*, 1978, *17*, 189–198.

Shapley, L. S. A value of *n*-person games. *In* H. W. Kuhn & A. W. Tucker (Eds.), *Contributions to the Theory of Games*, Volume 2. Princeton, New Jersey: Princeton University Press, 1953.

Shears, L. M. Patterns of coalition formation in two games played by male tetrads. *Behavioral Science*, 1967, *12*, 130–137.

Sherif, M. *The psychology of social norms.* New York: Harper, 1936.

Steiner, I. D. *Group process and productivity.* New York: Academic Press, 1972.

Sryker, S. Coalition formation. *In* C. G. McClintock (Ed.), *Experimental social psychology.* New York: Macmillan, 1972.

Tannenbaum, R., & Schmidt, W. H. How to choose a leadership pattern. *Harvard Business Review*, 1958, *36*, 95–101.

Taylor, M. *Anarchy and cooperation.* London: Wiley, 1976.

Vinacke, W. E. Sex roles in three-person games. *Sociometry*, 1959, *22*, 343–360.

Vinacke, W. E. Negotiations and decisions in a politics game. *In* B. Lieberman (Ed.), *Social choice.* New York: Gordon & Breach, 1971.

Vinacke, W. E., & Arkoff, A. An experimental study of coalitions in the triad. *American Sociological Review*, 1957, *22*, 406–414.

Willis, R. H. Coalitions in the tetrad. *Sociometry*, 1962, *25*, 358–376.

5

Improving the Problem-Solving Process in Managerial Groups[1]

L. RICHARD HOFFMAN

EDITOR'S INTRODUCTION

Through the theoretical framework called the hierarchical model, Hoffman in this chapter presents an integrated view of group decision making and problem solving. The model is a broad, complex one, resting on assumptions such as the existence of a tendency toward equilibrium in groups and identifiable stages in the process of reaching a group decision. However, through its use, some long-standing concerns of groups such as norms, the distinction between task-oriented and maintenance-oriented activity in groups, and the distinction between implicit and explicit activity can be addressed. The exposition of the model is clear, and Hoffman uses vignettes of group discussions in organizational settings to illustrate the theoretical points.

Of considerable importance to the model is the process by which alternative solutions to a problem accumulate valence, or attractiveness, in a group. Insights into this valence accumulation process, arising largely from

[1] This chapter was written while the author was visiting professor at the Graduate School of Management, Rutgers University and was supported in part by funds from the Interfunctional Management Program of that school.

Hoffman's own work, are given in the chapter, and the impact of this process on group decision and group member reactions are identified.

The hierarchical model buys us much with regard to understanding and improving group decision making. For one, as Hoffman shows, it can be used to interpret how certain well-known interventions for improving group decision making, such as brainstorming, have their effect. The model also suggests other, new ways of managing groups to make them more effective decision makers and problem solvers. These are discussed at the close of the chapter.

Managers in large organizations often have some form of the following discussion.

MANAGER A: *We never do any planning in this group. Everything is fighting fires.*

MANAGER B: *Look who's talking. All you ever do is take up our time with changes in the schedules and what that's going to mean for the guys in the warehouse. When you start thinking ahead, let me know.*

MANAGER C: *Aw, take it easy B. A is right, even if he doesn't do much to help us do it. If we did more planning for the entire operation, we wouldn't have so many schedule changes and fires to put out.*

MANAGER B: *Well, I agree, but I just don't have time for any more useless discussions like we had the last time we tried to plan. Everybody had lots of ideas for other people's operations, but they didn't want any changes in their own.*

MANAGER D: *Yeah, you guys all got on your high horse every time someone pointed out something wrong in your area.*

EXECUTIVE F (The Boss): *Okay. It sounds like you all want to have planning sessions and I think they would be very useful. Let's get together soon on that. I won't be able to meet next week, but let's schedule a meeting soon.*

Is this a problem-solving meeting? If so, how do we describe it? What is the problem the group is trying to solve? Can the group, as a whole, be considered to be solving a problem, or is each member solving a different one?

I suggest that the group was attempting to define a procedural problem, which each member labeled as "planning." The definition of the problem remained ambiguous and probably differed substantially from one member to the next. Some seemed to have long time horizons in mind, while others merely wanted to plan from week to week. Furthermore, the group has had bad past experience with the problem of planning. So the members successfully avoided adopting the problem for either this session or even for any foreseeable future.

Let us consider another fictitious example of a managerial meeting.

JIM: *Sally has asked that her desk be moved out of the aisle because people are always interfering with her work. I thought I'd get your approval before I did anything.*

JOE: *Where are you planning to move her? We gave that a lot of consideration before we put her there. I know you weren't in on that discussion, but finding the right spot for her was not easy.*

JIM: *Since she works so closely with Jerry, her supervisor, I thought I'd move her next to him.*

MARY: *Oh that would never do. What about Margaret? That's her spot and she's the head bookkeeper.*

JIM: *Yeah, but Jerry hardly ever needs her as immediately as he needs Sally. They're in almost constant contact all day long. Why can't Margaret and Sally switch places?*

JOE: *No. Mary's right. We can't switch Sally and Margaret. What is Sally's job anyway?*

JIM: *She's the account clerk on the XYZ account.*

MARY: *Then let's switch her with George. He won't be distracted by interruptions.*

JOE: *Yeah. That's an excellent suggestion.*

JIM: *But that would put Sally as far away from Jerry as she is now. As long as we are moving her, why don't we make it easier for her to work with Jerry?*

MARY: *Taking Margaret away from her present desk is out of the question. If Sally wants to get out of the aisle, switching with George is the only answer.*

JOE: *That's right. That's the only way.*

JIM: *I guess that's it if you guys say so, although I really don't understand. I'll tell Sally and George in the morning.*

Here again we find no explicit definition of the group's problem, but a solution is offered to the implicit problem of how to move Sally out of the aisle. That is the only problem that the group defined explicitly. However, alternate definitions of the problem are identifiable in the discussion: (a) Avoid interrupting Sally's work; (b) Increase her ability to interact with Jerry (the latter was never adopted by the group as part of the problem). Finally, one aspect of the problem was the one that weighed most heavily in the decision, but was never mentioned or recognized by one group member: (c)

Placement of the desks should never violate the status structure. Thus, an account clerk cannot be closer to the supervisor, Jerry, than the head book-keeper. That such an implicit definition of the problem can determine the outcome of a problem-solving session is a very common experience. Yet it is not described in any of the available models of group problem solving. Fur-thermore, there is no available model that recognizes that both of these discussions are problem-solving meetings with common characteristics. To help managers use groups more effectively, we must provide them with a problem-solving model that accounts for such phenomena. The hierarchical model is an attempt at a more comprehensive framework, geared to problem-solving groups in social contexts. In this chapter, I shall first review the origins of the model, describe its essential dimensions, and then show its utility for improving problem solving in managerial groups.

Studies of the Group Problem-Solving Process

PREVIOUS ORIENTATIONS

Until the development of the solution–valence theory and methodology to be described here, the specific content of problem-solving discussions has been relatively ignored. Systematic measurements of the process have fo-cused on the development of participation structures (Fisek & Ofshe, 1970) or on generalized task and socioemotional behaviors (Bales & Strodtbeck, 1951). While these are important aspects of group functioning, they ignore the principal phenomenon to be explained: the actual solving of problems by these groups. In that respect, I contend that such studies have not in-formed us about the basic problem-solving process and have often led us astray by their conclusions. I emphasize the word process because one of the principal conclusions to be drawn from the solution–valence studies is that the timing of events is often critical to the quality and acceptance of a group's decision.

Another line of research, typified by the work of James Davis (1973 and Chapter 3 in this volume), has attended to the content of the problem and has even made inferences about the decision-making process. But these studies have not examined the process directly. The typical study in this genre presents a group with a transcript of a jury trial and asks for a verdict. After determining the individuals' prediscussion judgments and the outcomes of the groups' deliberations, matrix manipulations permit the experimenters to test alternative hypotheses about the decision process used—unanimity, ma-jority, two-thirds majority, or some more complex rule.

Underlying such inferences are three assumptions of questionable validity. The first is that people's preferences remain constant throughout the course of discussion, that nobody is persuaded by the arguments of others in the group. Although people's beliefs are difficult to change, there is ample evidence that more people change to the group's decision than hold to their original judgment (Hoffman & Maier, 1961; Thomas & Fink, 1961). The second questionable assumption is that each member has an equal say in the decision. One person's vote counts as much as the next person's. While people may carry equal weight in formal voting procedures, some are more influential than others under most circumstances (Hoffman & Clark, 1979). And third is the assumption that only one decision is made by some simultaneous recording of the distribution of initial preferences. Ultimately, this last assumption is true. Each group must decide, for example, guilty or innocent, or fail to agree. But this decision may be trivial compared to the decision the group adopted concerning the credibility of a key witness about some piece of critical evidence. And that decision is never measured or even acknowledged by the experimenters.

One other approach to the problem-solving process has been a normative one. Recognizing that groups often produce inadequate solutions to problems—"a camel is a horse designed by a committee"—various procedures have been suggested for improving group effectiveness. Robert's Rules of Order (1943) are among the oldest of these and have been adopted almost universally in large parliamentary groups. However, many other techniques have appeared recently, ranging from the highly prescribed procedures of brainstorming (Osborn, 1957), nominal group technique (Van de Ven & Delbecq, 1971) and Delphi (Dalkey, 1969), to the loose principles and methods of Maier (1963) and Janis and Mann (1977). Of these, only Janis and Mann's recommendations derive from an overall theory, albeit a theory of individual decision making. The others are principally ad hoc attempts to overcome particular difficulties groups have in achieving effective solutions.

STUDIES OF THE PROBLEM-SOLVING PROCESS THROUGH SOLUTION VALENCE

The solution valence concept (Hoffman, 1961, 1979b) and the method for its measurement (Hoffman & Maier, 1964, 1967) were developed to remedy many of these shortcomings in the literature. Our experience told us that often the members' information about the problem was overlooked, rejected, or distorted during the discussion (Hoffman & Maier, 1961, Maier & Solem, 1952). Sometimes groups agreed early on a solution and were difficult to shake loose. Conflict was resolved creatively in some groups and became the source of hard feeling among the members in others (Hoffman, Harburg, & Maier, 1962; Maier & Hoffman, 1965). None of these experiences had been reflected in the studies of group process to that point. The phenomena described previously were observed during input–output experiments and actual discussions in ongoing groups, but not measured in systematic fashion.

Solution valence[2] is conceived as a force on the group toward (+) or away from (−) the adoption of a particular solution to a problem (Hoffman, 1961; Lewin, 1935). Each member also has valence for each solution. In fact, one or more members' valences for a solution may have signs opposite to the group's valence for that solution, even when that solution is the one adopted by the group. The likelihood that a solution will be adopted by a group is a positive function of its group valence. However, each member's commitment to that decision is a function of his or her individual valence (Hoffman, 1979b; Hoffman & Maier, 1964, 1967). Solution valence was operationalized successfully for several problems to permit us to track the process by which valence for various solutions accumulated, one was chosen, and members became differentially committed to it. While many of these studies have been reported in detail recently in *The Group Problem-Solving Process* (Hoffman, 1979b), a few results need to be highlighted for this discussion.

Figure 5.1 illustrates the valence history in one group of five possible solutions to a simulated personnel selection problem. The members were given five fictitious résumés and asked to select the best one for a hypothetical job. Because the group received the problem with very little time for the members to consider the résumés, there was no prediscussion valence for any candidates and all started at zero. Plotted in Figure 5.1 are the cumulative valence indexes generated during the group's deliberations. Time is represented on the abscissa.

Solution O, which was the solution adopted by the group, showed an early accumulation of valence past the adoption threshold, was essentially kept in reserve while other solutions were discussed, and then accumulated more valence while others were being discussed negatively. The first point to note is that the valence status of solutions will vary at different points in the group process, the solutions becoming more or less likely candidates for adoption by the group.

Table 5.1 shows the relationship between the final valence index achieved by solutions in 45 groups to the selection problem and in another 44 groups to a production problem. The relationships are very similar, clearly showing that increasing valence values were associated with greater

---

[2] In the hierarchical model, any cognition, belief, or value is presumed to have valence for both the group and its individual members: Definitions of the problem, goals of the group, norms about leadership. The empirical studies have been predominantly of solution valence. (Hoffman, 1979b; Stein, Hoffman, Cooley, & Pearse, 1979)

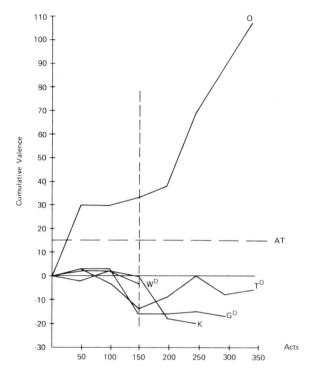

Figure 5.1. Solution–Valence Accumulations. Key: K, O, G, T, W = names of solutions; [D] = verbally discarded solutions; vertical line = announced end of rejection phase; AT = adoption threshold. O is adopted solution.

likelihoods of adoption. The second point is that the more valence a solution receives, the more the group is locked into that solution and resistant to entertaining new alternatives.

Point two is illustrated even more strongly by the dashed horizontal line at cumulative valence = 15 in Figure 5.1, which is labeled the "adoption threshold." No solution to either the personnel selection problem or the production problem was adopted without accumulating at least 15 valence points (see Table 5.1). Furthermore, the first solution to achieve 15 valence points was finally adopted in about two-thirds of the groups. Thus, in these groups we see clearly that once a solution has been favored publicly sufficiently often to pass the adoption threshold, it is unlikely to be unseated by any alternative. Typically under such circumstances, when a new solution is suggested, its weaknesses are immediately attacked—contributing negative valence to it—or the merits of the favored alternative are again enunciated, adding further positive valence to it.

TABLE 5.1
Valence Index and Adoption of Solutions

Valence index	Generative problem (N = 44 Groups) Percent of solutions — Adopted Principal[a]	Subordinate	Not adopted	Number of solutions	Choice Task (N = 43 Groups) Percent of solutions Adopted	Not adopted	Number of solutions
≥40	81.8%	6.1	12.1	33	80.0%	20.0	35
30 to 39	50.0%	16.7	33.3	12	58.3%	41.7	12
15 to 29	26.2%	35.7	38.1	42	36.4%	63.6	22
1 to 14	0.0%	2.6	97.4	302	0.0%	100.0	28
−9 to 0	0.0%	0.0	100.0	134	0.0%	100.0	52
−10 to −19	0.0%	0.0	100.0	1	0.0%	100.0	51
≤−20	0.0%	0.0	100.0	0	0.0%	100.0	15
Total				524			215

[a] Many groups, although asked to produce a single solution, solved the problem by combining two of our separately coded solutions as a single one, e.g., give the workers a bonus and train the foreman. In all but one instance one of the two solutions was described in great detail, while the other was added on, usually to satisfy a dissenting member. The detailed solution was labeled the Principal adopted solution and the other, the Subordinate.

The latter process can be seen in Figure 5.1. Between Acts 150 to 250, the valence of Solution T increased from −13 to 0, indicating that the group's discussion about T had been quite favorable during that period. Valence for Solution O, which had passed the adoption threshold during the first 50 acts and had leveled off at a valence of 30, showed only a modest response initially (between Acts 150 and 200) to the support for Solution T. However, as that support continued, valence for Solution O jumped by 30 points in the next 50 acts and continued that rate of increase to the end of the meeting, for a final valence of 110 points.

Lest the reader confuse solution–valence with the amount of discussion about the solution, a few points on that score should be noted. In the first place, the correlation between the total amount of discussion and the final valence for solutions (whether adopted or not) is only .26. However, when only the adopted solutions are examined, the correlations between valence and discussion, although far from perfect, are quite high (approximately .70). Typically, groups make many more comments about the adopted solution than about any other solution. However, a substantial amount of this discussion takes place toward the end of the meeting, well after the solution's valence index has almost guaranteed its adoption. Solution O in Figure 5.1, for example, received almost exclusively positive comments from Act 200 to the end, yet its adoption was assured, according to the valence index, well before that point. Furthermore, many solutions are discussed at length yet never accumulate any positive valence, like Solution T in Figure 5.1.

Similarly, the point at which the adopted solution passes the adoption threshold is unrelated either to the amount of discussion in the group generally or to the number of comments made about that solution in particular. In some groups, the adopted solution passed the adoption threshold within the first 60 acts, while others waited for 200 acts.

Not only does solution valence accumulate independently of the amount of discussion, but it also seems to be an implicit process. Groups are not aware of the valence status of solutions during the meeting, although their actions tend to reflect that status with a substantial lag in time. For example, in Figure 5.1 the vertical dotted line indicates a point at which the group ended its rejection phase explicitly (i.e., they declared that they had discarded the unacceptable candidates and were going to choose among the remainder). Solution O was retained and it had high valence. But Solution K was also retained, even though it had zero valence. From a valence standpoint, the group had already made its choice and, consistent with that prediction, Solution O, after that point, rapidly accumulated positive valence and was adopted. Yet it seems noteworthy: (a) that the group did not indicate in any way, at Act 150, that it preferred Solution O to Solution K; and (b) that it took an additional 200 acts for the group to actually make that choice.

Another aspect of the problem-solving process revealed by the solution–valence method concerns the relative influence of different members over the final decision. By disaggregating the valence accumulated for the adopted solution, we can identify the valence contributed by each member. Analysis of these individual valences results in two major conclusions: First, an individual's influence over the decision is only moderately related to his or her level of participation in the discussion. Especially in groups of size four and larger, the most influential member is often not the highest participant. Consistent with the previous conclusion that the valence adoption process is an implicit one, the contributions of the most influential member—especially the early support that pushes the solution over the adoption threshold—may be hidden behind the activity of a more vocal member (Hoffman & Clark, 1979).

Of equal importance is the finding that a member's satisfaction with the group's solution is positively correlated with his or her valence for that solution. The more positive things a member says about the group's solution, the more committed he or she is to it.

Both of these results have import for the difficult issue of the relationship between the individual and the group. We distinguish between the adoption of a solution, its quality, and its acceptance. Solution valence analyzed at the group level promotes a solution's adoption. The valence–adoption relationship holds no matter who causes the valence to accumulate—whether it is spread evenly among the members or whether one member dominates the others. Acceptance, however, is a function of the individual member's valence for the solution. He or she may also become committed to the solution if the group is attractive to him or her, but the member's valence for the group is a force added to solution–valence for his or her acceptance (Block & Hoffman, 1979). The quality of the solution bears no necessary relationship to these processes. The valence–adoption and acceptance relationships occur for solutions of both high and low quality (Hoffman & O'Day, 1979).

To produce a solution of high quality, a group must define the problem accurately, have relevant information available, use that information to support the adoption of the best solution, etc. Whether any or all of these events occurs is almost completely independent of the valence–adoption process per se. If, for example, the best solution accumulates the most valence, it will be adopted. But if the group ignores or distorts good information, a poorer solution will be supported and finally adopted.

These findings from our studies of the solution–valence aspects of the group problem-solving process have been summarized briefly to emphasize the need for a more adequate model of that process than presently exists. Certain points have been highlighted that serve as the cornerstones of the evolution of such a model. The hierarchical model is in its early stages of formulation and requires empirical testing of even some of its basic assumptions. I offer it here as a potentially useful framework—as a set of hypotheses if you will—for improving the problem-solving process in groups.

The Hierarchical Model

The hierarchical model is intended to be a depiction of the dynamics of the group problem-solving process. The static presentation in Figure 5.2, therefore, can only help to outline the general framework. The basic structure of the model consists of a boundary and three dimensions. The border around the figure represents the group's boundary. It identifies both the group's relevant task environment and the nature of its membership. The three dimensions are: (a) Task–Maintenance; (b) Explicit–Implicit; and (c) Normative–Localized.

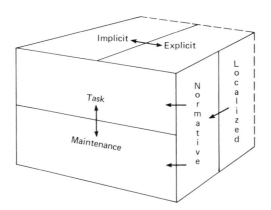

Figure 5.2.   Schematic illustration of hierarchical model.

THE GROUP BOUNDARY

The boundary is not, of course, a physical boundary, but rather a social fact (Durkheim, 1949). It defines who the group's members are, what the entry and exit requirements are, and how much commitment the members have to the group. Formal organizational groups may have quite impermeable boundaries (Hemphill & Westie, 1950), allowing inside only people of particular rank or those who are deemed by the group's leader to be relevant to the problem.

Even in such groups, however, members should be considered as only partially included (Katz & Kahn, 1978). They also belong to other groups, which may place conflicting demands on them. For example, the typical manager in a company is a member of his boss' staff, the leader of his own subordinate group, and often a member of a professional group, such as accountants or engineers, which impose standards of performance or conduct. Family obligations have become increasingly legitimate, so a manager can excuse him or herself from a meeting to meet a commitment to his or her spouse. In addition, each person retains an area of privacy which he or she is unwilling or unable to share with other members (Luft, 1969).

The size of the group is, then, only mildly approximated by the numerical count of bodies in attendance at a meeting. The willingness and ability of each member, singly and collectively, to commit his or her resources and energy to the problems of the group and its maintenance determine the effective size of the group. At one extreme, a group may have difficulty in even obtaining attendance at meetings and, once there, find members disappearing regularly. At the other extreme is a group in which each member is eager to participate openly in the meeting, is skilled in problem-solving methods, facilitates the contributions of others, commits to the group's decision, and pursues that commitment with enthusiasm.

The group's boundary is also defined in regard to the task environment. The group's manifest purpose determines what problems it is supposed to deal with. Sales executives consider problems of sales. A task force is assigned to study quality problems. Information may become available to a group but be rejected as outside its purview (outside its boundary). A middle-management group may recognize that a company policy is creating problems in its operations, but agree that the group has no power to change policy. Often the group's purpose is ambiguous and becomes defined only through experience. A task force assigned to study quality problems may look at the manufacturing organization generally or restrict itself only to deviations from standards.

A group's value and belief system also may be considered as part of its boundary. A group of engineering managers might view a problem in one way, while a group of marketing managers might see the same situation quite differently—the differences arising from their different professional experiences (Dearborn & Simon, 1958). The effectiveness of a group in coping with its task environment is often made difficult by the fact that people with similar backgrounds, personalities, or roles are likely to define a problem in only one way and miss possible alternatives (Hoffman, 1959). It is often only through legal requirements that an issue is forced into consideration by a group. Many executive groups denied the importance of integrating their work force until governmental agencies won costly discrimination suits against their companies.

The preceding discussion of the boundary recognizes the model's definition of the group as an open system in which many processes go on simultaneously. The boundary of a group may be more or less permeable to new information or to new members. But we assume that a group strives toward some quasi-stationary equilibrium (Lewin, 1947) with its environments and typically attains it for some time.

The equilibrium is maintained through habitual and regular interactions, which adjust easily to minor variations that occur in the environment. Groups develop formal procedures, such as rules for placing important items on the agenda. But common practices also become part of the group's method of adjustment (e.g., waiting for a senior member who is perpetually late).

A problem may be defined as a disturbance to the equilibrium that cannot be solved by the usual means. The disturbance may arise from either external or internal sources. A source of supply may be discontinued suddenly (task problem) or two of the members may get into a fight (maintenance problem). The disturbance creates the motivation to restore a state of equilibrium (i.e., to solve the problem) but the new equilibrium level may be different from the original one. The new level may be either an expansion of the boundary or a contraction. The boundary contracts when the group defends itself against an environmental incursion (e.g., by denying that the disturbance occurred or by having a member become alienated and withhold important resources from the group). The boundary expands if the group develops a novel solution to the problem, which gives it greater control of the environment, or if the group facilitates increased cooperation and snyergy among the members.

Note that the problems described in each case concern transactions across the boundary as well as problems arising in the group. Recognizing that problems can arise for a group in either area leads to the first dimension of the model: Task–Maintenance.

TASK-MAINTENANCE DIMENSION

Following Bales (1953), we divide the processes by which the group solves problems into two major categories: task and maintenance. Task functions deal with the manifest purpose of the group: accomplishing its functions in the organization. The maintenance functions are concerned with holding the group together, facilitating the members' ability to cooperate with each other, and gaining the members' commitment to the task of the group. Both the task and maintenance functions are activated when a group comes into existence, and they operate simultaneously while the group is functioning. For example, as the group attempts to solve its task problem, people may become angry or frightened at the conflict that erupts. There may be subsequent consequences for the quality of the decision reached, the members' commitment to it, and the cohesiveness of the group (e.g., Hoffman, Harburg, & Maier, 1962).

EXPLICIT–IMPLICIT DIMENSION

Crosscutting the task–maintenance dimension is the dimension of explicitness. The model assumes that either task or maintenance problems are being attended to explicitly at any particular time, but not both. However, whichever one is being considered explicitly, the other is occurring implicitly. We see this parallelism clearly in laboratory studies of group problem solving. While the group solves the experimenter-imposed task, a social structure emerges, as shown by the stable, but unequal, rates at which members participate (e.g., Fisek & Ofshe, 1970; Kadane & Lewis, 1969). As the members define the problem and suggest solutions, they develop implicit norms about turntaking, dominance relationships, etc.

Team-building activities in organizational groups offer a contrasting example of explicit attention to maintenance functions. While team building is designed to improve the members' ability to interact, task issues are often worked on in these discussions. One member might say to another, "I didn't believe you at all the other day, when you said you would get the Cramer report to me by Friday. Your tone of voice suggested that you hadn't even started on it." In response, the other might say, "I can understand why you felt that way, because I wasn't quite sure whether I could overcome one snag. Maybe it would be better if I share my doubts with you rather than have you distrusting me. We did overcome that snag, by the way, so you'll have it on Friday as promised." While feelings of trust are worked on, information about the report is also communicated. Members' commitments to their group's decisions—made at the task level—often reflect their feelings about the process by which the decision was reached. The point I stress here is that while the group is solving its task problem, maintenance functions are also being performed at an implicit level and, less frequently, vice versa.

The model posits that the explicit problem of the group dominates the implicit functions. By dominate I mean that when issues are made explicit by the group, they are treated as legitimate topics for discussion and come under the self-conscious control of the members. Other issues that affect the group are kept at an implicit level, where their interpretation is more ambiguous. For example, in the case of moving Sally's desk, described in the introduction, the group discussed possible locations for Sally at the explicit level, but left to the implicit level the issues of status as a criterion and which member has the ultimate authority to make the decision. It is not unusual for decisions to be made on implicit criteria that are not discussed, especially if the power relationships in the group are clearly understood.

NORMATIVE–LOCALIZED DIMENSION

The third dimension of the hierarchical model is called normative–localized and it, too, crosscuts the other two dimensions, (see Figure 5.2). The normative dimension is least understood despite the large body of theoretical and empirical literature extant on the topic of norms. The model assumes that norms develop to regulate the behaviors of the group members to replace the need for direct interpersonal control (Thibaut & Kelley, 1961). However, it also recognizes the fact that all behavior in a group is not normatively controlled. At the localized extreme of the dimension, each person behaves somewhat idiosyncratically, reflecting his or her personality, external role, or, even, temporary mood. At other points along the dimension are such phenomena as stereotypes (i.e., expectations about the behavior of a particular member) and coalition formation, in which the norms for some subset of the group are different than they are for others.

While recognizing that this treatment of norms is a gross oversimplification of the topic, there are two distinctions produced by the crosscutting of this dimension with the other two in the model that are worth noting. The first is the fact that norms exist both for task and maintenance functions. We are accustomed to thinking about norms concerning participation, turn-taking, expressions of emotionality, and even norms about discussing norms (Argyris & Schön, 1974) as part of the maintenance process. However, the procedures by which a group solves a problem may also have normative qualities. The various techniques that have been invented to facilitate problem solving—Osborn's brainstorming, Maier's screening principles, Dalkey's Delphi method—have explicitly stated rules to which the members must conform. As with maintenance norms, the members understand what they are to do more or less well and conform differentially.

The other important distinction arises from the relationship between the normative dimension and the explicit–implicit one. This aspect of the model recognizes that some norms are stated explicitly ("Everyone will be at this meeting on time") or, more often, violations are clearly sanctioned ("Let's keep the tone of this meeting businesslike."). Explicit norms are like Goffman's (1974) "frames," in that they define the general character of the meeting. His ingenious analysis of such phenomena is consistent with the present treatment. Especially noteworthy is his recognition that frames may be created by certain members—implying the appropriateness of particular norms—so those members can manipulate the group to their personal ends.

Other norms operate implicitly. They become effective through the reinforcements they receive during the discussion (Jackson, 1960). Merely seating him or herself at the head of the table assures a person recognition as the leader, and a subsequent pattern of dominating the other members will cause them to defer to the "emergent leader" without any specific references having been made to his or her assuming that role (Stein, Hoffman, Cooley & Pearse, 1979). Often such norms arise exogenously and merely need one or two instances of confirmation in the group to become operative. Especially when the norm prohibits certain behaviors, their nonoccurrence in the group confirms the existence of the norm.

One other point needs to be made about implicit norms. Because they are not discussed, and are often normatively not discussable, (Argyris & Schön, 1974), each person's concept of the norm may be quite different (Jackson, 1960). The events that define the norm will be interpreted individually according to the motives, perceptions, etc. of each member (Kelley & Thibaut, 1978). For these reasons, norms often lead to dysfunctional consequences for the group and are difficult to change.

THE PROCESS MODEL

The dimensions of the model are useful for highlighting the multiple-processing aspects of group functioning. A problem-solving group is not just working on its manifest task, but is simultaneously resolving maintenance issues as well. The greater utility of the model, however, lies in the processes that underly these dimensions.

The valence concept helps us understand the dynamic aspects of the hierarchical model, for it provides us with a way of describing the forces on the group at each of the several levels defined by the crosscutting of the three dimensions. Both because this chapter is concerned primarily with solving problems in managerial groups and because we know more about the task level of the model, Table 5.2 will be useful in bringing the model to one more level of specificity. There we see the well-accepted, if empirically unverified, stages of a problem-solving session. The group is assumed to have the potential of moving from defining a problem and specifying its character, through generating and evaluating possible solutions, to, finally, selecting and implementing one of them, thus reestablishing its boundary with the environment. Several qualifications must be made immediately.

TABLE 5.2
Task-Level Stages in the Problem-Solving Process

Defining	Specifying	Generating	Evaluating	Implementing
General nature of problem	Barriers to be overcome	Alternative solutions	Solutions	Solution adopted
Goals to be achieved	Criteria to be met	Characteristics of candidates	Candidates	Solution adopted
————————→		————————→	————→	————————→

One is to recognize that any problem may have more or fewer than these five stages, depending in part on the complexity with which it is defined by the group. One group might see a problem of shift work as caused strictly by low wages and decide to raise the shift differential. Another might see the problem as one concerned with both the physical and mental health of the shift workers. That group might attempt to design a new shift schedule and provide social facilities at times when the evening and night workers can benefit from them. The second group would, presumably, have many more stages than the first one.

Second, the model does not assume that a group must go through all the stages. In fact, many problems are solved inadequately because the problem is presented to the group at the generating or even the evaluating stage, and the problem subsequently is never well defined. The problem of moving Sally's desk is a typical example. Essentially the group was moved quickly to the solution-evaluating stage by Jim's statement, "I thought I'd move her next to him (her supervisor)." This statement stimulated negative evaluations by the others. One other solution was offered and adopted without ever really defining the problem completely. No wonder Jim concluded, "I really don't understand." Thus, a problem may enter the group at any stage.

Furthermore, the model posits a force toward restoring the boundary, which tends to move groups toward evaluating and selecting solutions and away from defining and specifying problems. This force is an implicit norm, analogous to Maier's (1963) contention that groups tend to be "solution minded." It is represented by the arrows in Table 5.2.

Groups are assumed to move from one stage to another in either of two ways. At the implicit level we have already seen that groups select solutions through the solution valence adoption process, moving in that way from the generation and evaluation stages into the implementation stage. An analogous process is assumed to occur at earlier stages as well, abetted by the general force moving the group to the implementing stage (Hoffman, Bond, & Falk, 1979). The latter force allows the group to move to the generating–evaluating stages by accumulating only modest valence for any problem definition.

The group may also change stages explicitly, as when the leader says, "I think we have enough possibilities, let's pick the best one now." He is calling on the group to move from the generating to the evaluating stage and using his power to ensure the move.

The group may also move backward by an explicit declaration, "I think we ought to hold off on suggesting solutions until we've defined the problem." Implicit valence for the group's entrance into the generating stage may thus be overruled by such an explicit statement. However, if the valence for the generating stage is already high—either because valence for the implicit problem definition was high or because the group had spent considerable time and effort in suggesting and evaluating solutions—the directive to return to the problem-defining stage might be rejected ("We all know what the problem is!").

Groups may also fail to move forward due to conflict at the implicit level. If the valences for two or more solutions have both passed the adoption threshold and are of approximately equal magnitude, an impasse may be reached. One resolution of that impasse would be a search for another alternative (moving back from evaluating to generating) or even an attempt to define the problem better so the merits of both alternatives can be recognized (moving from evaluating back to specifying). Such conflict can generate creative solutions to problems (Hoffman, 1961).

Conflict is often resolved, however, by intruding maintenance norms on the problem-solving process. An acknowledged expert may be given the floor to expound at length on the merits of his or her preferred alternative, thus increasing its valence to a level beyond successful attack. The inexpert opposition may be reluctant to challenge the expert, although their own negative valence for the solution may reduce their commitment to it.

Similarly, the formal leader of the group may indicate his preference or merely prevent the group from reconsidering the problem by saying, "We've spent enough time on this issue. Let's make a choice." If the leader has substantial power (i.e., the group has high valence for the leader's being powerful) the group will refrain from moving backward and attempt to make the designated choice.

The first example in the introduction, of the group calling for planning, provides another illustration of norms of power affecting the outcome. Although valence was accumulating implicitly for using the group for planning, the boss's failure to set a time for such a meeting was an implicit signal that he did not really want a planning meeting. The group's valence for his power was sufficiently high, compared to their valence for wanting a planning meeting, that his statement cut off any additional discussion. The meeting ended without any change in the group's inability to plan. In terms of the model, the boundary was restored to its old equilibrium position.

One final point regarding a group's movement from stage to stage is implied by the distinction between the adoption and acceptance of a solution in the studies of solution valence. Adoption is a function of group valence, while acceptance is a function of individual valence for the solution. In similar fashion, when a group moves implicitly from one stage to another, only certain of the more vocal members may have contributed to that movement, while others either remain at the earlier stage or reluctantly or resentfully move with the group. Members may withdraw from further discussion or merely go through the motions of participating, if they feel that their views of the problem, for example, were not given a fair hearing by the group. Group leaders are often surprised when they learn much later that one member "thought the whole idea was crazy from the beginning." From the viewpoint of the hierarchical model, the group was diminished in size to the extent that this member's resources were withheld from the group. Even when the movement from one stage to the next is made explicitly, all members may not accept the shift. However, unless the norms of the group permit such objections to be verbalized, they may have the same negative effect on the quality and acceptance of the final decision.

THE ACCUMULATION OF VALENCE

How does valence accumulate? In the first place, all valence accumulations are implicit, although there may be a dramatic positive shift in valence values as an issue is moved from the implicit to the explicit level. (The relationship between the implicit and explicit levels is one of the most problematic aspects of the model and is currently being studied in one aspect of leadership.) Valence for a belief accumulates through rewarding and punishing experiences in the group. While we assumed successfully in the solution–valence studies cited earlier that the groups started the discussion with zero valence for all solutions, we recognize that in most real life groups there is substantial valence for many relevant beliefs.

These result from the group's own previous experience, as well as from the members' previous socialization with the organization and in society generally. For example, we learn that a formally appointed leader has legitimate power to direct a meeting. So a group is likely to have high valence for a previously unknown but legitimately appointed leader's engaging in a variety of directive, task-facilitating acts. Positive valence for that person in the leadership role accumulates as his or her behavior is consistent with the implicit norm. The valence may become so positive that the leader can extend the range of acceptable behavior. Negative valence may accumulate, however, if the leader's behavior is inconsistent with the norm. If the leader antagonizes members or insists on a particular way of solving the problem, his or her valence as leader may drop so low that he or she is displaced informally or is, in fact, deposed (Hollander, 1978).

In real organizational groups, the leader's valence is usually very high as a result not only of his or her legitimate power, but also of his or her ability to provide rewards and punishments, and often his or her technical expertise (French & Raven, 1959). Such a leader has great difficulty in utilizing the group's resources, unless he or she uses his or her power to facilitate the members' participation in the discussion. Since the valence for the leader's power is ordinarily so great, the leader need make very few overt acts to confirm to the members that opposing the leader would be a very risky endeavor. Thus, while the curves for the accumulation of solution valence increase slowly in Figure 5.1, we can assume that in ongoing groups, the valences for a variety of norms are at very high positive or negative values at the outset and are continually confirmed in the several meetings of the group (Hoffman & O'Day, 1979).

To change the norms of an established group requires one to recognize the experiential basis for these high values. Therefore, for a previously auto-cratic leader to become more participative would require the group to experi-ence such a leadership style sufficiently frequently to overcome their valence for the leader's autocracy. A mere announcement by the leader of an in-tended change in style will be ineffective in changing such valence unless his or her behavior supports it consistently and does not regress into old habits.

Even more difficult to change are those norms that were established on a punitive basis and have such high negative valence that the behaviors never occur. Many groups are stymied by the fact that admitting weakness or error in the group subjects the confessor to great abuse and ridicule. Such a group finds few problems to solve, since the norm of hiding problems pre-vents such information from crossing the boundary to be considered by the group. An outside observer unacquainted with this history might assume from listening to the group's discussion that all is well in the group's world. Even when the members of such a group have become so paralyzed that they want to change, they often have no way of changing, since such a group is also likely to have a norm against discussing inadequacies in their own group process.

To change norms with high negative valence requires the creation of a safe climate in the group for expressing behavior deviant from the norm. An explicit announcement by the group leader that recognizes the faulty norm helps reduce the negative valence somewhat. The leader's own admission of fault to the group through specific examples would reduce it still further. Usually such unilateral action by the leader requires substantial counseling with him or her privately before the meeting to reduce his or her anxiety about the likely negative consequences of such a confession.

Related to the accumulation of valence for beliefs through the rewards or punishments experienced in their expression is the accumulation of valence for new behaviors, especially new skills. Old methods are comfortable, even though they may be recognized as ineffective or wasteful. New methods are often awkward. At the least they usually restrict the autonomy of the mem-bers, since they are designed to interfere with old habits. For example, it is usually impossible to prevent a group leader initially from offering rebuttal to unacceptable beliefs expressed by subordinates on his or her first attempt. Only after he or she has received feedback on his or her deviations from the new norm of accepting all ideas does he or she begin to conform more easily to the new norm and to suppress the rebuttals. The group, too, must learn the new methods and stop censoring ideas that the members know will antagonize the group leader. As the group practices the new method and experiences success with it, it becomes easier to do and acquires valence as a group norm.

Applications of the Hierarchical Model

Of what practical use is the hierarchical model to the improvement of group problem solving in organizations? The model has two advantages. First, it provides an integrative framework that has been lacking in the field of group dynamics (Zander, 1979). I shall analyze a number of methods that have been proposed—frequently as panacea—to improve the problem-solving effectiveness of groups to determine what functions they perform according to the model. Second, the model alerts us to aspects of the process that provide opportunities for improvement or present risks to the group. The opportunities should be recognized and appropriate methods adopted to capitalize on them. The risks must be attended to or they may produce undesirable outcomes for reasons that are not obvious to the group members (i.e., the causes are implicit). In both cases, I shall assume that the reader wants to help the group arrive at the best solution to the problem with maximum commitment by the members.

METHODS

Brainstorming.   Osborn's (1957) attempts to improve the creativity of his advertising staff evolved into the brainstorming method. Fundamental to its use is the "principle of suspended judgment"—the postponement of evaluation during the period of idea generation. The value of this method within the hierarchical model is two fold. First, the members' efforts are concentrated first on developing a roster of possible solutions, then on their evaluation. In this way no solution can acquire enough positive valence to pass the adoption threshold nor enough negative valence to drop below the rejection threshold before many alternatives have been proposed and described. By having a procedure—a task norm—that permits only the proposing of alternatives, the members feel secure in searching for new ideas without fear that their current favorite will be discarded. Members can be proactive rather than defensive in their approach to problems.

The hierarchical model also suggests that brainstorming can be used for defining the problem as well as for generating solutions. By shifting the question from "What might be done?" to "What possible causes are there for this situation?", the technique can facilitate an accurate definition of the problem.

Nominal Group Technique (NGT). This method (Delbecq, Van de Ven, & Gustafson, 1975) adds another dimension to the separation of idea generation and idea evaluation. Studies of brainstorming groups show a tendency to limit solution proposals to particular directions. Such limits would be expected in the hierarchical model if a particular definition of the problem becomes adopted implicitly during the brainstorming session. Even though many different solutions may be proposed without evaluation, the problem they are designed to solve may develop substantial valence in the group, thus making other problem definitions more difficult to recognize.

The NGT attempts to release the total creativity of the group in two ways. First, group members are required to develop solutions to the problem individually, without consulting each other. In this way, each member's perspective on the problem enters the group's problem-solving efforts uncontaminated by the others' points of view. No valence for a particular definition of the problem can then exist before all solutions have been presented.

Second, each member is required to contribute one solution to the group in turn or to pass his or her turn. This procedure continues until all solution possibilities have been exhausted. In this way, every member's idea has a chance to enter the group's deliberations without having to fight its way in (Hoffman and Clark, 1979; Thomas & Fink, 1961). New solution possibilities can still "piggyback" on the suggestions of other members during this phase, yet the valence for a particular problem definition is unlikely to have as limiting an effect in NGT as in straight brainstorming. Furthermore, as in brainstorming, when the group enters the evaluation phase, all proposed solutions have minimum amounts of valence and have a reasonable chance of being adopted.

The principal advantage of NGT over brainstorming in the solution proposal stage is its defense against the participation and influence biases that derive from the personalities or statuses of the members (Hoffman, 1965; Berger, Cohen, & Zelditch, 1972). Such biases, representing intrusions of the maintenance level on the task functions, are often negatively correlated with the determinants of high quality decisions (Torrance, 1955).

Delphi Technique. The Delphi Technique (Dalkey, 1969) was designed primarily for noninteracting groups. However, besides its obvious advantages for groups whose members are geographically distant, one of its principal objectives is to minimize the effects of status differences on the decision-making process. In its simplest form, the method asks each member of the group to make an independent and anonymous judgment on a pre-defined problem. These judgments are then averaged, giving each person's judgment equal weight. The members are then told what the average and the distribution of judgments were and asked to vote again. Reasons for different votes may be included in the report. This process may be repeated again if necessary to promote consensus.

The principal advantages of the Delphi Method are two related ones. First, the anonymity of the votes and their equal weight prevent the higher status members from having undue weight on the decision. On the assumption that all members of the group have relevant information, the intrusion of maintenance factors on the decision is then reduced. The second advantage is that there is an explicit, easily understood mechanism for making a final decision, which avoids the biases of the implicit valence adoption process.

By avoiding any discussion of the problem among the members, however, the Delphi Technique runs two risks. The first is a lack of understanding of the problem and of the final decision. There is an implicit demand for conformity to the majority created by the noninteractive process of collecting judgments. It is difficult for a group to adopt a truly creative solution to a problem through the Delphi Technique, since the ideas of the minority are not usually clarified (Delbecq, Van de Ven, & Gustafson, 1975).

The second risk is the lack of members' commitment to the decision gained from expressing one's personal support for the decision. The members whose preferences are deviant from the majority's are expected to comply with the decision, even though they have not been convinced of its merits (Delbecq, Van de Ven, & Gustafson, 1975).

Identifying the Essential Conditions.   The Likerts (Likert & Likert, 1978) recommend an additional step after a group attempts to define the problem. This step is the listing of "essential and desirable conditions [p. 428]" for a solution to the problem. These conditions are those aspects of the solution that each member believes are needed from his or her personal perspective. After these have been listed without objection, the group attempts to gain consensus on a list of absolutely essential conditions.

This method thus moves the implicit assumptions the members are making about acceptable outcomes to the explicit level at an early stage in the process. In the ordinary free discussion, solutions to a problem are offered and evaluated and gain valence beyond the adoption threshold. At the same time the members become polarized around the implicit valence for the conditions they feel are essential to a solution. It is difficult at that point for such conditions to be discussed in a dispassionate and problem-solving manner. Rather, the conflict may be joined in a win–lose fashion (Blake & Mouton, 1961).

The Likerts' method causes the group to confront these differences early, before the group develops valences for opposing conditions and becomes polarized. They suggest that such confrontation can be resolved more cooperatively at that point and problems with potential for strong latent conflict can be solved more easily.

This brief analysis of some of the methods presently recognized as useful could be extended, but I hope its objective of illustrating the specific functions these methods perform has been met. There are no panacea; just more or less powerful methods for overcoming difficulties or facilitating opportunities. The hierarchical model provides a framework with which to analyze other methods for improving group problem solving to determine their particular usefulness toward that end.

ADDITIONAL PRINCIPLES DERIVED FROM THE HIERARCHICAL MODEL

New Methods Meet Resistance.   The methods described in the previous section provide two examples of useful derivations from the hierarchical model. In the first place, all such methods involve new behaviors and orientations by the members. Brainstorming, for example, requires people to be willing to sound silly by offering outlandish ideas. People are used to censoring such thoughts, lest they lose status in the group.

The members are likely to resist any method that restricts their freedom to act habitually, especially when the required behaviors oppose those habits. The new behaviors have to be learned, so practice sessions are needed. The more successful applications of these methods have occurred in groups that had been trained in their use (Maier & Hoffman, 1960; Parnes & Meadow, 1959). With success, the valence for the method will increase and make it an established norm.

Resistant attitudes are especially likely when there is distrust in the group. Each technique, neutral though it may be, may be seen as a manipulative device in the hands of a mistrusted leader. The boundary of the group becomes impermeable to new information and methods as the members defend themselves against being harmed. Maier's (1963) risk technique, in which members express their doubts and fears about the new method, may be helpful in converting such defensiveness into a willingness to try the method without total commitment.

The corollary of the principle that methods may be resisted from mistrust of the group is that methods are best introduced in a climate of trust. The more members trust each other, the more open they are to viewing new techniques accurately. The members are more willing to take risks, being able to predict that the other members will not abuse them if they fail.

The level of trust in a group is a fundamental property of the group's maintenance. It develops as a function of continuous experiences by the members with each other in almost every aspect of the group's activity. Probably one of the most potent destroyers of trust is the leader's mistaken belief that if an issue is avoided, it will not affect the feelings of the members. Many times executives are unwilling to admit that a costly mistake has been made, even to the people who were most closely involved. In so doing, they sacrifice a level of trust, which can have continuing consequences in members' doubts about future executive pronouncements.

Compose the Group Appropriately. Boundary issues also arise when the group is being formed. What is the purpose of the group and who should attend its meetings? Meetings are such time-consuming and often aversive events that people are often pleased to be excused, so they can do their "real work." A manager will often say, "Well, this is a production problem, so you guys in marketing and accounting don't have to attend the meeting." Or an executive will decide that he wants to discuss a problem with Joe and Sam individually, even though the problem involves them jointly. He has found in the past that each of them will be more open with him without the other one there, so he has more information to work with.

From the point of view of the hierarchical model, in both instances the decision as to who should attend the meeting is based on a narrow interpretation of the group's task. The task is only to get the immediate decision made as quickly as possible. No consideration is given to the possibility that the quality of the solution might benefit from the ideas of others. Successive one-on-one discussions with Joe and Sam concerning their joint problem sacrifice the potential stimulation they might receive from each other. The production problem might benefit from the perspectives of those less directly involved.

The model also alerts us to more subtle effects of these practices. Several implicit messages are sent to those who might have attended the meeting. First of all, the leaders' attitudes toward such meetings are communicated. The production manager indicates that meetings are a waste of time and should be minimized. Joe and Sam's boss indicates that he wants to control his relationship with each of them privately. He may be showing his distrust of them, as well as modeling for them how to keep their subordinates under control. Instead of increasing the capabilities of these people to operate as a group, these managers have arrested that potential by preventing the group from working together on the problem.

Finally, as in many such situations, there is no recognition of the use of the problem-solving group for the individual development of the members. Since it is a production problem, the accountant, personnel manager, and marketing manager lose the opportunity to learn about production problems by being excluded.

New and Deviant Ideas Must be Encouraged.   One of the principal implications of the solution-valence studies is that a solution must accumulate valence beyond the adoption threshold to be truly a candidate for adoption. However, once one solution's valence has passed that threshold, the group has difficulty entertaining other alternatives. Furthermore, the more valence the original solution accumulates, the more difficult it is for new ideas to be introduced successfully. Of course, solutions that fit habitual directions in thinking are most likely to accumulate valence readily.

One way of preventing the dominance of familiar solutions is to separate the idea-generation from the idea-evaluation stages (Maier, 1963) to prevent the members from evaluating any suggestions until the group has exhausted all possibilities (Osborn, 1957). In this way, all alternatives can be considered and understood by the group before any substantial valence has become attached to one of them.

Since creative ideas do not always appear on call, but rather arise from some hidden recesses of the mind or from some fortunate juxtaposition of ideas, a member may produce such an idea after the generation phase is over. To insure that such an idea has a chance to be adopted, the group must encourage the speaker to elaborate on the details and virtues of the idea. The group members, too, should attempt to identify the advantages of the new idea. In this way, valence for the new idea can pass the adoption threshold and be considered seriously along with the other alternatives.

In general, then, all new solutions should be examined for their merit so they can accumulate maximum valence before their possible disadvantages are mentioned. This procedure is especially important where other solutions may have passed the adoption threshold already, since there is a strong tendency then to search immediately for reasons to reject the newcomer.

Maier's (1963) principle of "protecting minority opinions" is also consistent with this concept. Minority opinions often have difficulty being considered seriously by a group because the majority are set to reject it. For example, a minority of one in a four-person group may add one valence point for his or her new idea, but each of the other members could add a negative valence point in response, resulting in a net value of minus two (one minus three). It is no wonder, then, that the majority tends to prevail, right or wrong (Hoffman & Maier, 1961; Maier & Solem, 1952). If the majority can learn to examine the virtues of the minority opinion, that opinion might accumulate enough valence to challenge the dominant opinion and be considered seriously by the entire group. Maier and Solem (1952) showed that merely instructing the leader to make sure that all opinions were heard decreased substantially the ability of an incorrect majority to dominate the correct minority member.

Avoid Pseudoconsensus. The implicit valence–adoption process often produces a seeming consensus when only a few members favor the action to be taken. However, those in favor tend to be the most vocal members and the others remain quiet in the belief that they are alone in their objections. Failure to raise such objections in the group can have two negative consequences. First, the silent objector will lack commitment to the idea and even sabotage it if he or she feels overriden by the majority (Hoffman & Maier, 1959). Second, to the extent that the objection is based on relevant facts, the group may adopt an inadequate solution. By failing to capitalize on the objecting member's information or to acknowledge his or her interpretation of the facts, the group may adopt an unworkable solution to which only some of the members are committed.

The importance of gaining true consensus is even greater at the earlier phases of the problem-solving process, when the group is attempting to define the problem. Maier's (1963) precept that "the starting point of a problem is richest in solution possibilities [p. 241]" is often overlooked as the group adopts the problem as originally stated. Especially when the boss defines the problem in a particular way, he or she is often deaf to any attempted redefinitions. The valence for that definition quickly becomes so high, as solutions are offered to it, that members who differ with that definition withdraw from the discussion or merely participate passively in the charade—"Let's solve the boss's problem." Again, the possibility of a poor solution with low acceptance looms high.

To assure consensus requires a norm of openness to objections and conflict at each stage of discussion. The "principle of suspended judgment" (Osborn, 1957) must not only be applied to solutions, but also to problem definitions. "Checking out"—by which I mean asking for each member's point of view before moving on to the next stage—is essential for avoiding pseudoconsensus. Checking out requires more than mere assent to such questions as, "Does everybody understand? Nobody objects, do they?" Such questions merely invite conformity. More potent would be "What do you think the risks are of such an action? What are the advantages, as you see them?" Such questions require the member to explicate his or her view of the matter and gain the respondent's commitment to the action. Even the question about advantages often reveals the member's doubts, either through outright omission of a discussed advantage or through hesitancies and doubts in his or her statements. These can be explored in the group if the group's norms make it safe to object or to delay the group's progress toward a solution. At the least, checking out ensures that everyone is in agreement on the same solution before they try to implement it.

Make Assumptions Explicit.   Discussions of alternative solutions often generate valence for both solutions without recognizing that each is attempting to solve a different problem. In our studies of a problem of underproduction, groups often debate the merits of installing an incentive system versus redesigning the job layout. They may even mention that the incentive scheme will cause the workers to work harder, while the job redesign will capitalize on the workers' manifest abilities, implying that they are arguing about solutions to two different problems. However, rarely does a group examine the evidence for the existence of each of the problems. Rather, advocates of the incentive solution argue that "Everybody wants more money" or "I worked in a shop with incentives and everybody worked their tails off," while job redesign is supported on similar grounds unrelated to the case at hand. Such unwillingness to postpone the evaluation of solutions until the problem has been defined explicitly and the group's consensus has been gained as to its true nature illustrates Maier's (1963) contention that groups are too "solution minded." To define the problem at that point in the discussion would require a seeming step backward, and groups seem generally reluctant to do that. In the hierarchical model, this reluctance is represented by the valence attached to "restoring the boundary" by adopting a solution.

In laboratory groups, such reluctance is often enhanced by personal power plays whereby some member becomes so invested in dominating the group that he or she (typically, he) stubbornly insists on his solution to the point where the others withdraw from the fray (Hoffman & Clark, 1979). Such intrusion of personal needs on the problem-solving process illustrates the effects of maintenance functions on the task level in the model. Unfortunately, I have never heard anyone in such groups say explicitly, "Oh John, you just want to have things your way. That's why you won't go along with our idea," thus making the reasons for the group's difficulty explicit. Poor solutions might then be avoided after John's power needs had been dealt with.

Making the implicit assumptions explicit in managerial groups, while often desirable for solving a particular problem, is often fraught with such risks for the status of the member that it is rarely seen. A common occurrence will illustrate my point. A vice-president of production in a company might suggest to his department heads that a task force be appointed to identify the ways in which marketing causes inefficiencies in the plants. The boss's definition of the problem of inefficiencies clearly restricts the purview of the task force. Yet, while the group discusses instances of inefficiencies it becomes clear that many of them could be solved within the production department and some were even due to policies set forth by the vice-president.

When a department head suggests that the task force should look into all sources of inefficiency, the group is immediately told by the vice-president that the task force is limited to the impact of marketing. When the department head persists, the vice-president becomes furious at him, makes a personal attack on his ability to manage his own area, and reaffirms the limited mandate of the task force. It is easy to see from an external perspective that the vice-president's purpose in establishing this task force is not to reduce the inefficiencies in the production department. He has limited the group's ability to solve that problem by using his power to overcome the members' efforts to broaden the definition. If any of the department heads were to make explicit his or her sense that the production vice-president was preparing a power play against the marketing vice-president and not really concerned with reducing inefficiencies, he might risk being fired. In this company, department heads are supposed to understand such motives, but not to express them publicly—an example of a powerful implicit norm.

Conclusion

My intent in this chapter has been to describe an evolving model of the functioning of problem-solving groups that will be useful for facilitating their effectiveness. The model's usefulness in analyzing existing methods and in suggesting new practices should encourage managers to think more productively about the potential of such groups and how they might operate more effectively.

I would like to make two more points in concluding the chapter. First, despite the intent of the model to facilitate our understanding of the problem-solving *process,* there is still a strong structural overtone to the treatment. The notion that there are dimensions to the process and the mechanics of the methods described is intended to provide a context for that process, not to cast the process into some mechanical format. There is no substitute for the leader's and member's sensitivity to each other and to the needs of the group at any particular time. The interpersonal competence (Argyris, 1962) and leadership skills (Maier, 1963) emphasized by other authors are central to the effective use of this model.

Finally, the model is, of course, evolving and highly speculative in many parts. Research supports many of the propositions already, but others have not been examined at all. Probably the most difficult issue for tests of the model is attempting to determine the level of valence for implicit norms, values, and beliefs. Therefore, the model is offered as a heuristic, a way of thinking about problem-solving groups in an integrated way, but far from the final word.

References

Argyris, C. *Interpersonal competence and organizational effectiveness*. Homewood, Illinois: Irwin-Dorsey, 1962.
Argyris, C., & Schön, D. *Theory in practice*. San Francisco: Jossey-Bass, 1974.
Bales, R. F. The equilibrium problem in small groups. *In* T. Parsons, R. F. Bales, & E. A. Shils (Ed.), *Working papers in the theory of action*. New York: The Free Press, 1953.
Bales, R. F., & Strodtbeck, F. L. Phases in group problem solving. *Journal of Abnormal and Social Psychology*, 1951, 46, 485–95.
Berger, J., Cohen, B. P., & Zelditch, M., Jr. Status characteristics and social interaction. *American Sociological Review*, 1972, 37, 241–255.
Blake, R. R., & Mouton, J. S. *Group dynamics—key to decision making*. Houston, Texas: Gulf, 1961.
Block, M. W., & Hoffman, L. R. The effects of valence of solutions and group cohesiveness on members' commitment to group decisions. *In* L. R. Hoffman, *The group problem-solving process: Studies of a valence model*, New York: Praeger, 1979.
Dalkey, N. C. *The delphi method: An experimental study of group opinion*. Santa Monica, Calif.: The Rand Corp., 1969.
Davis, J. H. Group decisions and social interaction: A theory of social decision schemes. *Psychological Review*, 1973, 80, 97–125.
Dearborn, D. C., & Simon, H. A. Selective perception: A note on the departmental identification of executives. *Sociometry*, 1958, 21, 140–144.
Delbecq, A. L., Van de Ven, A. H., & Gustafson, D. H. *Group techniques for program planning*. Glenview, Illinois: Scott, Foresman, 1975.
Durkehim, E. *Division of labor in society*. Glencoe, Illinois: The Free Press, 1949.
Fisek, M., & Ofshe, R. The process of status evolution. *Sociometry*, 1970, 33, 327–46.
French, J. R. P., Jr., & Raven, B. The bases of social power. *In* D. Cartwright (Ed.). *Studies in social power*. Ann Arbor, Michigan: Institute for Social Research, University of Michigan, 1959.
Goffman, E. *Frame analysis*. New York: Harper & Row, 1974.
Hemphill, J. K., & Westie, C. M. The measurement of group dimensions. *Journal of Psychology*, 1950, 29, 325–42.
Hoffman, L. R. Homogeneity of member personality and its effect on group problem-solving. *Journal of Abnormal and Social Psychology*, 1959, 27, 27–32.
Hoffman, L. R. Conditions for creative problem solving. *Journal of Psychology*, 1961, 52, 429–444.
Hoffman, L. R., & Maier, N. R. F. Valence in the adoption of solutions by problem-solving groups: Concept, method, and results, *Journal of Abnormal and Social Psychology*, 1964, 69, 264–271.
Hoffman, L. R. Group problem solving. *In* L. Berkowitz (Ed.). *Advances in experimental social psychology* Volume 2, New York: Academic Press, 1965.
Hoffman, L. R., & Maier, N. R. F. Valence in the adoption of solutions by problem-solving groups. II. Quality and acceptance of goals of leaders and members. *Journal of Personality and Social Psychology*, 1967, 6, 175–182.

Hoffman, L. R. Applying experimental research on group problem solving to organizations. *Journal of Applied Behavioral Science,* 1979a, *15,* 375–391.

Hoffman, L. R. *The group problem-solving process: Studies of a valence model.* New York: Praeger, 1979b.

Hoffman, L. R., Bond, G. R., & Falk, G. Valence for criteria: A preliminary exploration. *In* L. R. Hoffman, *The group problem-solving process: Studies of a valence model,* New York: Praeger, 1979.

Hoffman, L. R., & Clark, M. M. Participation and influence in problem-solving groups. *In* L. R. Hoffman, *The group problem-solving process: Studies of a valence model.* New York: Praeger, 1979.

Hoffman, L. R., Harburg, E., & Maier, N. R. F. Differences and disagreement as factors in creative group problem solving. *Journal of Abnormal and Social Psychology.* 1962, *64,* 206–214.

Hoffman, L. R., & Maier, N. R. F. The use of group decision to resolve a problem of fairness. *Personnel Psychology,* 1959, *12,* 545–559.

Hoffman, L. R., & Maier, N. R. F. Sex differences, sex composition, and group problem solving. *Journal of Abnormal and Social Psychology,* 1961, *63,* 453–456.

Hoffman, L. R., & O'Day, R. The process of solving reasoning and value problems. *In* L. R. Hoffman, *The group problem-solving process: Studies of a valence model,* New York: Praeger, 1979.

Hollander, E. P. *Leadership dynamics.* New York: The Free Press, 1978.

Jackson, J. M. Structural characteristics of norms. *In* National Society for the Study of Education, *The dynamics of instructional groups.* Chicago: University of Chicago Press, 1960.

Janis, I. L., & Mann, L. *Decision making.* New York: The Free Press, 1977.

Kadane, J., & Lewis, G. The distribution of participation in group discussions: An empirical and theoretical reappraisal. *American Sociological Review,* 1969, *34,* pp. 710–722.

Katz, D., & Kahn, R. *The social psychology of organizations* (2nd ed.) New York: Wiley, 1978.

Kelley, H. H., & Thibaut, J. W. *Interpersonal relations.* New York: Wiley, 1978.

Lewin, K. *A dynamic theory of personality.* New York: McGraw-Hill, 1935.

Lewin, K. Frontiers in group dynamics: Concept, method, and reality in social science, social equilibria and social change. *Human Relations,* 1947, *1,* 3–42.

Likert, R., & Likert, J. G. A method for coping with conflict in problem-solving groups. *Group and Organizational Studies,* 1978, *3,* 427–434.

Luft, J. *Of human interaction.* Palo Alto, California: National Press Books, 1969.

Maier, N. R. F. *Problem-solving discussions and conferences: Leadership methods and skills.* New York: McGraw-Hill, 1963.

Maier, N. R. F., & Hoffman, L. R. Using trained "developmental" discussion leaders to improve further the quality of group decisions. *Journal of Applied Psychology,* 1960, *44,* 278–283.

Maier, N. R. F., & Hoffman, L. R. Acceptance and quality of solutions as related to leaders' attitudes toward disagreement in group problem-solving. *Journal of Applied Behavioral Science,* 1965, *1,* 373–385.

Maier, N. R. F., & Solem, A. R. The contribution of a discussion leader to the quality of group thinking: The effective use of minority opinions. *Human Relations,* 1952, *5,* 277–288.

Osborn, A. F. *Applied imagination.* (Rev. ed.) New York: Scribner, 1957.

Parnes, S. F., & Meadow, A. Effects of "brainstorming" instructions on creative problem-solving by trained and untrained subjects. *Journal of Educational Psychology,* 1959, *50,* 171–176.

Robert, H. M. *Robert's rules of order.* Chicago: Scott Foresman, 1943.

Stein, R. T., Hoffman, L. R., Cooley, S. J., & Pearse, R. W. Leadership valence: Modeling and measuring the process of emergent leadership. *In* J. G. Hunt and L. L. Larson (Ed.), *Crosscurrents in leadership.* Carbondale, Illinois: Southern Illinois University Press, Leadership Symposium Series, Volume 5, 1979.

Thibaut, J. W., & Kelley, H. H. *The social psychology of groups.* New York: Wiley, 1961.

Thomas, E. J., & Fink, C. F. Models of group problem solving. *Journal of Abnormal and Social Psychology,* 1961, *68,* 53–63.

Torrance, E. P. Some consequences of power differences on decision making in permanent and temporary three-man groups. *In* A. P. Hare, E. F. Borgatta, & R. F. Bales (Eds.) *Small groups: Studies in social interaction.* New York: Knopf, 1955.

Van de Ven, A. H., & Delbecq, A. L. Nominal versus interacting group processes for committee decision-making effectiveness. *Academy of Management Journal,* 1971, *14,* 203–212.

Zander, A. The study of group behavior during four decades. *Journal of Applied Behavioral Sciences,* 1979, *15,* 272–282.

6

Creativity, Groups, and Management[1]

MORRIS I. STEIN

EDITOR'S INTRODUCTION

The capacity to be creative is an asset to any group engaged in making decisions and solving problems. It is something, though, often regarded as mysterious in origin and unmanageable in practice. In the following chapter, Stein counters this view. He sheds light on the nature and nurture of the creative process and suggests ways of heightening the creativity of decision-making groups in organizational settings.

Some concepts of the same name have quite different characteristics when examined at the individual and group levels. For example, the concept of decision rules, when used with reference to groups, typically refers to choice processes of majority rule, unanimity, and so forth, while the concept used with reference to individuals typically refers to processes of choice based on dimensional comparison among alternatives or maximization of utility. Creativity, however, is a concept of identical elements when addressed at the individual and group levels of analysis, as Stein makes clear in this chapter. In fact, the creativity of a group is largely seen as a direct product of the creative capacity of the individuals in it. Consequently, the understanding

[1] The work reported here was supported through a Career Award (5K06-MH 18679) from the National Institute of Health.

and management of group creativity requires an extensive knowledge of individual creativity.

Stein delineates the creative process early in this chapter and proceeds to survey its development and use in social contexts, especially in the organizational realm, and the chapter closes with a discussion of recommendations for enhancing the creativity of individuals and groups in organizations.

Just as there are actors in search of an author, so there are decision-making techniques in search of creative decision makers. That is the relationship between this chapter and those that precede it. While they concern themselves with the hows and the whys of decision making, this chapter focuses on those making the decisions, as well as a special subgroup: those who make creative decisions. These are people who not only generate unique problems, but who also engage in events of low probability and high payoff (Lederberg, 1980), and arrive at decisions that contain original solutions and novel paradigms (Kuhn, 1970) that have significant effects on our perception of the environment around us and our adaptation to it.

There are times, however, and those we are living in now may be some of them (Nisbett, 1980), when creative persons might well be an endangered species. Pressures for conformity, antirationalism, restricted research funds, unclear administrative practices, etc., all combine to make for a worrisome picture.

My purpose in this chapter is to help hold the fort against these pressures by: (a) calling attention to the current threat; (b) describing the nature of the creative process, the characteristics of the creative individual, and the social context in which the process occurs; (c) discussing the role of the manager as an intermediary in the creative process; and (d) concluding with a series of recommendations to help provide a more effective relationship between management and creative persons in any one company.

The Current Threat

Based on my studies of the creative process among research people employed in industry, I have prepared a list of 10 commandments for them.

1. They are to be assertive without being hostile or aggressive.
2. They are to be aware of their superiors, colleagues, and subordinates as persons, but not to become too personally involved with them.
3. They may be lone wolves on the job, but they are not to be isolated, withdrawn, or uncommunicative. If they are any of these, they

had best be particularly creative so that their work speaks for itself.
4. On the job they are expected to be congenial, but not sociable.
5. Off the job they are expected to be sociable, but not intimate.
6. With supervisors they are expected to "know their place," without being timid, obsequious, submissive, or acquiescent.
7. But they are also expected to "speak their minds," without being domineering.
8. As they try to gain a point, more funds, or more personnel, they can be subtle but not cunning.
9. In all relationships, they are expected to be sincere, honest, purposeful, and diplomatic, but never unwilling to accept "shortcuts," or be inflexible or Machiavellian.·
10. Finally, in the intellectual area, they are expected to be broad without spreading themselves thin, deep without becoming pedantic, and "sharp" without being overcritical (Stein, 1963, p. 124; 1974, p. 261).

The stress and strain involved in fulfilling these commandments are often so great that one wonders why anyone even opts for creativity.

There seems to be something about creative persons that people see as threatening. This is manifest not only at the adult level, but also with children. Children who score high on creativity tests are regarded by their classmates and teachers as "naughty," "silly," and as having "far out" ideas (Torrance, 1962). The creative child usually finds him or herself under pressure to be less productive and less original. When he or she makes good contributions to the successful completion of the group's goal, he or she may not be given proper credit. Group members may sanction their most creative member and control his or her behavior by openly expressed hostility, criticism, ridicule, rejection, indifference, or isolation. In grades five and six, Torrance tells us, "organizational machinery" may be used to control the creative child. Such a child may be elected to an administrative position or made recording secretary so that he or she is kept busy with the group's minutes and has no opportunity to make any contributions to the group's endeavor (Torrance et al., 1964).

Parents have organized to help their creative children cope with the "pain of being different." One such parent filed a lawsuit against the school that said that his creative child was a behavior problem and wanted to put him in a behavior modification program. In the same article, Dr. Harold Lyon, director of the United States Department of Education's Office of Gifted and Talented, is quoted as saying that creative children are "our most valuable resource and often our most neglected one," and Marie Friedel, executive director of the National Foundation for Gifted and Creative Children, says, "This country seems to want to treat creativity as a pathological affliction [Bennett, 1980]."

Returning to the adult level, we find that in recent years, and probably as a function of a declining economy, the problems of the creative individual are exacerbated. In 1976, a vice-president of a major chemical company said that when he joined his company as a chemist some 25 years ago, he was given free rein "to create." Now that he is in charge, he says he would like to tell his own researchers "to create" but he cannot. His company "is finding research projects too costly to support and is cutting back on many of its innovative, exploratory programs." The company killed a third of its long-term medical research projects and closed down one unit completely (Bronson, *The Wall Street Journal,* 1976).

The same article reported that "Surveys taken by the chemical industry show that chemical companies' research and development investment this year [1976] will reach $1.36 billion, compared with $800 million a decade ago. But this year [1976] a far greater percentage of the total spending is going into modifying products already on the market, for competitive reasons or to satisfy government health and safety regulations. Far less money is going to the development of new products." The article then concludes with the statement that "company executives say the long-term results will be an 'innovation shrinkage.'"

The prophecy was quite accurate, for the Joint Economic Committee of Congress in 1976 reported that "The average American is likely to see his standard of living decline in the 1980s unless we accelerate the rate of growth of our nation's productivity." And, in 1980, a news item entitled "Will the Slowdown in New Product Introduction Continue?", we find an ad agency reporting that "new grocery and drug offerings fell 2.8% last year after declining 1.7% in 1978" (*The Wall Street Journal,* 1980).

Put all of this in the context of a culture characterized by narcissism (Lasch, 1979) and the possible disappearance of progress as a value (Nisbett, 1980) and the future indeed looks dismal, both for the creative individual and for those managing him or her. Today, managers are challenged more than ever to meet this threat. To succeed, they need to learn not only how they themselves can make more effective decisions, but also how they can protect and foster the development of our economy's most precious resource for making creative decisions—creative people. To aid in this regard, we begin with a discussion of what is known about the process through which these people work, follow it with a discussion of their various psychological and social characteristics, and conclude with a discussion of management's relationship to such people and some recommendations for future efforts.

This chapter may not contain all that needs to be known in this area; hopefully, it will suffice as a starter.

The Creative Process

Creativity is a process that results in a novel work that is accepted as tenable, useful, or satisfying by a significant group of others at some point in time. It involves the transformation of previously existing materials or ideas and their integration into a form that did not exist before. The novel end product is accepted, first, by some relatively small group of significant persons, and, in time, by larger and larger groups in the society. The creative work is adaptive and–or it provides a new paradigm (Kuhn, 1970) for understanding and dealing with the world around us.

The creative process is the general case for achieving novelty. Other processes—serendipity, discovery, etc.—are subsummed under it. The creative process accomplishes more than do these other processes. It starts with a greater leap into the unknown; its end product is more "distant" from that which existed previously; and it yields a more inclusive paradigm.

One of the first descriptions of the creative process was presented by Helmholtz (Whiting, 1958). It was built upon by Poincaré (Whiting, 1958) and elaborated by Wallas (1926) who called the stages of the creative process by the now familiar terms: preparation, incubation, illumination, and verification. Reichenbach (1938) took a somewhat different tack and differentiated between two contexts—the *context of discovery* and the *context of justification*. Kris (1952) differentiated three phases: inspiration, elaboration, and communication. He is one of the few who speaks of *communication* directly and is in accord with my own tripartite description of the process as consisting of three stages—*hypothesis formation, hypothesis testing,* and the *communication of results*—which I have discussed at greater length elsewhere (Stein, 1963, 1967, 1974b, 1975), and which I shall discuss briefly here.

HYPOTHESIS FORMATION

Hypothesis information follows a period of preparation during which the creative individual spends a great deal of time or intensive short periods in either formal or informal training and education. Hypothesis formation itself begins with some problem formulation, no matter how tentative, and extends to the development of ideas or hypotheses that can be tested.

The problem as it is first formulated does not usually lend itself to an immediate solution. Indeed, it is because there is no immediate solution that there is any problem at all. It is, therefore, necessary to restate the problem in a manner that will make it more amenable to solution. One must take a *problem as given* and transform and reorganize it into a *problem as understood*. This may sound tautological. It is not. Creative persons seem to have a knack, more frequently than do others, for stating problems in such a manner that they are amenable to creative solutions.

There are a number of theories as to what motivates creative people to seek out problems. To discuss these theories is beyond the scope of this chapter. Suffice it to say that the creative individual is motivated to make disorder out of existing order, in order to make a better order (Barron, 1958).

It is still unknown just how a hypothesis occurs to an individual. Even introspectionist psychologists, using fractionalist methods, can come up only with the suggestion that an idea occurrs through a process of unconscious inference, following various associations. The concept, "unconscious inference," however, is more descriptive than explanatory. Although details are missing, it is assumed that much unconscious work does go on in the formulation of ideas or hypotheses. Incubation may occur and an idea "rises" to awareness. Sometimes full conscious awareness is not evident; the creative individual simply, "reflexively," unconsciously, and without awareness, makes a selection.

Conceivably, the idea selected is related to a feeling of inspiration or simply feeling good. It provides direction to the creative individual's later activities.

Some persons go no further than hypothesis formation. They may lack in motivation, discipline, time perspective, or some other characteristic necessary for developing their ideas further. Nevertheless, they may be important to the creative process by calling the attention of others to a problem or to a significant area of work. These people take satisfaction in being "idea men." Still others may be unable to do much with their ideas because they are too angry, too negativistic, too critical, or even feel too inadequate. All these and others do not get to the next stage—hypothesis testing.

HYPOTHESIS TESTING

A salient characteristic of the second stage of the creative process is testing and evaluation. Ideas that vary in degrees of tentativeness are checked out to determine whether they are useful and can be implemented.

After the artist conceives of an idea for a painting, he takes brush in hand and works it out at his easel. The composer, hearing a tune in his head, goes to the piano, and plays the notes to see how they combine realistically. Scientistis test ideas in controlled laboratory experiments. Theoreticians conjecture about their hypotheses and do checks on their logical status. But testing in reality, in vivo, may have to take a good number of years.

All this makes the hypothesis testing stage sound determinate and structured. This is not so, for this stage is characterized by many fits and starts. As T. S. Elliot said, "Between the conception and the reality lies the shadow."

As the creative individual moves from hypothesis formation to hypothesis testing he shifts his roles. During hypothesis formation he is *subject*. He is the one who comes up with ideas and selects from amongst them the one that he will test. During hypothesis testing, however, the creative individual is both *subject* and *object*. He does something as subject and then becomes his own audience viewing his work as object—as others might see it. The ebb and flow of this activity yields refinements in the work and the "shadow" that previously existed is gradually dissolved.

The end of hypothesis testing is marked by the novel product, which the creative person finds elegant enough and satisfying enough because it meets his requirements and criteria. Because there is some tangible product and because the creative person is satisfied, many persons regard the creative process as finished at this point. Others, like myself, believe that the fruits of creative labor have yet to be presented or communicated to others for their acceptance or rejection.

COMMUNICATION OF RESULTS

Just as the creative individual alters his or her perspective from subject to object in moving from hypothesis formation to hypothesis testing, so another change happens as the move occurs from hypothesis testing to the communication of results. During the last stage of the creative process, "others" become salient. These others are those who will respond to, evaluate, criticize, accept and–or utilize that which has been produced. Previously, these others might have been in the back of one's mind, but now they take center stage. The creative individual might only need to consider how these others are best communicated with. On other occasions, depending on the nature of the final product, changes might have to be made in the character of the work so that others can accept it.

Einstein tells us that the manner in which the theory of relativity occurred to him was not the manner in which it was presented in the Einstein–Infeld book (Wertheimer, 1945). In talking about the presentation of the work, Einstein said, "No man thinks in such a paper and pencil fashion." It has to be presented that way so that it can be understood by others.

While "others" always figure, to some extent, in the creative process, the degree to which this is so is a function of a number of factors. Chief among them is the role the creative person sees for him- or herself and the role he or she attributes to the audience or public. The creative person who sees him- or herself as expositor or teacher may consider others to a greater extent than does the creative person who sees him- or herself as seer, prophet, or developer of new perceptions and new paradigms. Technical jargon is used with groups of experts and lay terms are used with the larger audience or public.

The communication stage is also effected by the character of the work. The acceptance of innovations by the public are effected by the innovations' "relative advantage, compatibility, complexity, trialibility, and observability" (Rogers & Shoemaker, 1971), the characteristics of the media used to communicate the product, and the characteristics of the target audience whose members vary in their readiness to adopt novelty (Stein, 1974b).

Because the communication stage of the creative process requires special skills and abilities that the individual who is capable of hypothesis formation and hypothesis testing may not possess, society has established special roles to carry out these functions. To the people who carry out these roles, I have given the name of *intermediaries,* because they fulfill such important functions between the originator of the idea and product and the audience or public at large. In the broader society, intermediaries are: the patrons of the arts, the critics, the reviewers, the curators of museums, etc., all of whom play crucial roles in determining whether the creative work will be presented to an audience or public. By their evaluations—criticisms, published or otherwise, they influence the response to a work.

The value of intermediaries for the creative process is often denigrated by persons who do their best in hypothesis formation and hypothesis testing. Such an attitude is unfounded as is shown by many case studies of creative works that succeed as well as studies of those that fail.

The creative process, only some of whose most salient characteristics I have described here, does not run off smoothly from beginning to end. Boredom, fatigue, not knowing how to proceed, may all block or impede the process. Incubation and unconscious work goes on while the creative individual turns from his or her work to other matters. But he or she has·to be ready to accept new awarenesses that illuminate new directions and move the process closer and closer to a creative solution. Feelings of depression may occur as well as feelings of excitement and exhilaration. These latter are often associated with "inspiration." There are moments in which cognitive awareness and affective feelings concur in responding to a work. These are the moments of aesthetic sensitivity that signal that a work is nearing completion or is already complete.

The novelty of the final work must be of some significance. Novelty in some insignificant detail, while noteworthy, does not merit being called creative. Novel results need to be "useful, tenable or satisfying" (Stein,

1967) or "adaptive" (MacKinnon, 1964). The result must be a "leap," not a mere step away from that which existed. The creative result changes the course of future actions and behavior. It alters our perceptions of the world. It provides us with a new paradigm (Kuhn, 1970) and opens new vistas that stimulate further creativity.

The Creative Individual

Who is the individual who seeks out and is capable of fulfilling the requirements of the process just described and making creative decisions? What are his or her psychological characteristics? This is not merely a theoretical question, the answer to which would yield fascinating information about a very interesting and unique individual. It is also a practical matter. To be able to describe the creative individual or to be able to differentiate him or her from lesser creative persons means not only that one knows what one is looking for, but also that there are techniques available to make such selections and differentiations. For the manager in industry, this means that he or she has available aids to help in the selection of creative decision makers. In this regard, we are further along now than we have ever been. As with all other techniques, constant improvements and refinements are always necessary. Where it is not feasible to use selection techniques themselves, it is possible to utilize the results for phrasing interview questions and so maximize the probability of selecting the persons one needs.

The material to be presented is based primarily on my colleagues' and my research with chemists, all of whom were involved in industrial research, employed in research and development (R & D) departments and divisions of several major companies on the American scene. Holding education constant, they were all Ph.D.s, and with age being approximately the same, our task was to differentiate between those men who were regarded as "more creative" from other men in the same organizations who were regarded as "less creative." Judgments as to creativity were made by subordinates, peers, and supervisors.

While the major part of that which will be presented is based primarily on this study, some data selected from the literature will also be presented. Let us turn now to data from three areas: biographical, personality, and cognitive. Due to space considerations, only certain highlights can be discussed.

BIOGRAPHICAL CHARACTERISTICS

There are so many experiences that a person may have during the course of his or her lifetime that it is surprising that one can find any life history variable that differentiates creative people from others. This is especially true if one controls subjects' gender, educational status, age, and general field of work, as we did in our study.

Much, but not all of the data to be presented, are statistically significant. Those that are not are very close to acceptable standards and they derive further importance from the manner in which they relate to each other and to various data in the literature.

The more creative men in our study come from families where there seems to be a tradition of creativity, a value on creativity, and role models that fostered orienting oneself to creative pursuits. A significantly larger proportion of the more creative than less creative persons we studied said their grandparents were creative. The grandparents might not have met Galton's (1870) standards for hereditary genius, but they did fulfill rather gross criteria. A grandfather might have been known as "a fantastic carpenter, who could make anything" and a grandmother could have been known as "a creative seamstress and even better known for her embroidery." None of these achievements set the world on fire, but, no doubt, they were part of a family tradition and value system that implicitly stated "people in our family do creative things." Simultaneously, they suggest the possibility that models were available to our subjects when they were youngsters and these models could nurture and shape the careers of those who were to become creative.

Data obtained from our subjects also indicated that the parents of our more creative subjects were different from those of the less creative ones. The former, we were told, had goals for their sons. They wanted their sons to be "something," just what did not matter. On the other hand, a larger proportion of the parents of the less creative men did not have goals for their sons. Taken in conjunction with the data provided on grandparents, there is now further support for the suggestion that our creative subjects grew up in families that provided structure for their sons' potential by emphasizing the importance of goal-oriented behavior.

The data just presented on parents and grandparents may make it sound as if the more creative persons in our study had smoother sailing in their lives than was true of the less creative men. If so, then consider some life history data with regard to parental consistency and life complexity.

One of the questions asked of our subjects was how consistent they thought their mothers were while they themselves were youngsters. We were rather surprised when data obtained from the more creative men indicated that they thought their mothers were *less* consistent than was true of the less creative men. This datum suggests two possibilities of interest insofar as future creativity is concerned. To have perceived less consistency in their mothers' behavior suggests the possibility that their mothers were not always there to serve, care for, and fulfill their sons' needs. If so, this could have led to the son's learning how to draw upon and utilize his own resources if he wanted to satisfy his needs. If he was successful in such behavior, he could have learned he was capable and regarded himself with esteem. Consequently, he would be more likely to be confident in future ventures—even to explore novelty and be creative.

The fact that the mother was not always consistent might well have had at least one other important consequence. It is conceivable that the mother's level of consistency could reflect her own autonomy and independence. She did not feel she had to deny her own needs to provide sameness and consistency for her son. By allowing herself opportunity to fulfill her own needs, she provided her son with a model for autonomous and independent behavior—characteristics that would stand him in good stead in his future creative career.

Let us now turn to another matter—that of complexity. Here again, we learn some interesting data. While both the more and less creative men we studied said they experienced about the same degree of complexity in their lives—that is, experienced a serious illness or disability, had to adjust to a new environment because the family moved, there was a death in the family, etc.—what did differentiate between the two groups of subjects was their reaction to this complexity. The more creative men had more "positive" reactions and the less creative men had more "negative" ones. More of the less creative men said they *withdrew from* or had *depressive reactions to* the complexity they experienced, while more of the more creative men said they were *challenged* or *stimulated by* the complexity they experienced.

Were these experiences related to the differences between our two groups of subjects in dealing with the complexity of creative work? Surely there are lots of pieces missing in the jigsaw puzzle. We don't know all the steps between early experiences with and reactions to life complexity. Such experiences, however, might well make a fertile foundation for responses to future complexity. As Hofstadter (1979), in his work on *Gödel, Escher and Bach* points out, it is the more complex oyster, "a complex living beast whose innards give rise to this mysteriously simple gem"—the pearl. So the individual who experiences complexity and is not afraid of it, who is even challenged and stimulated by it, may, with the added help of a family tradition that values creativity and contains models for autonomy and independence, be the person who later in life seeks out and solves problems creatively.

PERSONALITY CHARACTERISTICS

The literature and our own work is replete with mention of personality characteristics that characterize creative persons or that differentiates them from less creative individuals. A sample (Stein, 1968, 1974b) reveals that the creative individual is: achieving; has a need for order; is high on curiosity; is self-assertive, dominant, aggressive and self-sufficient; rejects repression; is less conventional and low on authoritarianism; is persistent and self-disciplined; is independent and autonomous; has little interest in interpersonal relationships; is intuitive and empathic; is less critical of himself than others are of themselves; makes a greater impact on others, etc.

Once again, the manager seeking creative persons might do well to keep these characteristics in mind during recruitment interviews or, if the opportunity avails, itself, to use appropriate psychological services and procedures for such purposes.

COGNITIVE CHARACTERISTICS

No doubt creative persons share many cognitive characteristics with other people, but they also *differ* from others in at least two ways for which we have data. One of these is in the area of perception and the other is in the area of problem solving. They seem to have more of a certain characteristic way of perceiving the world around them and the *process* through which they solve problems is different from that utilized by their lesser creative colleagues—even though both groups do solve the problem.

Turning to perception first, we found in a specially designed test that has since been published (Stein, 1974) that the more creative men in our study gave somewhat more evidence of perceiving stimuli physiognomically than was true of less creative individuals. Physiognomic perception involves perceiving objects as if they possessed animate or human-like characteristics. A good example of this comes from the artist Kandinsky's biography, in which he tells us that he sees paints as raindrops on his palette "puckishly flirting with each other," and how they come together as "sly threads" and "roguishly skip about . . . [Werner, 1957, p. 17]."

Physiognomic perception appears earlier developmentally than do other forms of perception. Most persons lose their capacity for physiognomic perception, but creative persons, capable of what some psychoanalysts call "regression in service of the ego [Hartmann, 1964]" still use this perceptual style in their adult lives. In so doing, they are capable of greater perceptual flexibility and achieve a greater variety of perceptual mixes. Less creative persons, persons not so capable of physiognomic perception, are more likely to be rigid and less capable of combining that which they see into new forms.

Physiognomic perception results in what may be regarded as perceptual metaphors, and, like other metaphors[2], it can go a long way in facilitating the course of the creative process. Physiognomic perception is not only a cognitive control variable, but in some respects it can also take its place along with other important nonrational and alogical processes, such as day- and night-dreaming, which have also played crucial roles in the creative process.[3]

Along with differences in perception, creative persons differ from their less creative colleagues in the *process* through which they solve problems. The emphasis here is on the word *process*. In the problem-solving experiment utilized, aprroximately the same number of more and less creative men solved a given experimental problem. The *product* did *not* differentiate between the two groups of men, but as we shall see, the *process* did. This is consistent with the principle of equifinality in General System Theory (von Bertalanffy, 1968). Following this principle, the same solution to a problem can be arrived at by persons following different pathways to the solution.

The problem (John, 1957) was one that could be solved logically and rationally. A running account was kept of the subject's problem-solving process (Blatt & Stein, 1959). The data were anayzed following a Gestalt model (Wertheimer, 1945) and consisted of three phases: an analysis phase (where data were gathered), an intermediate but shorter lag phase (where there is some milling about), and an integration phase (where the available information is pulled together and the individual goes to solution). Using this model, we found that the more creative men differed from their less creative colleagues in that they asked more of their questions and spent more of their time in the analysis phase and consequently asked proportionately less questions and spent less time in the integration phase. Using T. S. Elliot's metaphor, cited previously, of the *shadow* that lies between the *conception* and the *reality,* we think that the creative person is able to dissolve something of the shadow by the problem-solving process he or she utilizes. Unlike less creative individuals, the more creative one "feels out" the component parts of a problem and then integrates the information obtained. He behaves

[2] There are numerous instances where metaphors played important roles in the creative process. The Wright brothers studied buzzards in flight to solve problems in balancing airplanes; Brunel, for his work on the caisson, studied the boring behavior of the shipworm; Bell used the mechanism of the inner ear for his work on the telephone; Kekülé used the image of the snake chasing its tail for his study of carbon atoms. Gordon (1961) presents these and other instances of metaphors in creative work. He utilized various forms of metaphors for his creativity-stimulating technique *synectics*.

[3] A list of such instances may be found in Brown and Luckcock (1978). I am indebted to Dr. Joshua Lederberg for calling my attention to this paper.

very much like a good pinball machine player whose body sways with the moving ball as it bounces off the bumpers and with appropriate body English makes the ball go to the appropriate slots in the machine so that he racks up a big score and wins points.

The less creative person, on the other hand, plays the game as if he were manning a machine gun. He behaves explosively, emitting random bursts. He tries to grab hold of what seem to be response patterns, but which are meaningless more often than not. Should he grab hold of a correct pattern, he is surprised that it works and cannot repeat it because he does not understand it nor how it came about in the first place.

Since our study of the problem-solving behavior of more and less creative individuals, Blatt (1961) utilized the same apparatus to gather other very interesting information. He studied subjects' physiological responses, especially heart-rate, during the course of the problem-solving situation. Because each of the subject's attempts to gather data was impressed on a moving tape, it could be correlated with sequential physiological data. The pattern of physiological responses, it was found, reflected crucial characteristics of the problem-solving process. Thus, as the individual came close to the end of the analysis phase in the problem-solving process, there was an increase in heart rate. What was more interesting about this was that neither experimenter nor subject knew where in the problem-solving process the individual was. These data were available only after the experiment was over and the data were analyzed.

Finally, Blatt also found that just before the subject attained solution to the problem, heart rate also increased. Once again, the subject was unaware, at least consciously, that he was close to solution. Is it possible that there is a level of "physiological awareness" that some persons do not make use of because they are not sensitive to it or because other, more conscious, factors interfere? Is it possible to train people to be sensitive to their physiological responses and so facilitate their problem-solving efforts and their creativity? Gordon (1961) suggested that it would be a good idea if one could be more aware of the hedonic tone of experiences while seeking creative solutions to problems. On the basis of Blatt's work, we tend to agree.

It is far beyond the scope of this chapter to present at length all of the biographical, personality, and cognitive characteristics that characterize the creative individual and differentiate him or her from their less creative colleagues. Let the presented material suffice to make the point that variables have been found in all three of the aforementioned areas that are related to creativity. Managers are now in a position to use both techniques and information for the recruitment of creative persons and to better understand those already on the job.

The Social Context and the Creative Process

Thus far, we have limited ourselves to a discussion of the *intra*personal aspects of the creative process. The process, however, is not limited to what goes on within the individual. Creativity is also effected by *inter*personal factors—those that exist at the macrolevel of the culture and those that exist at the microlevel of the group.

THE CULTURE

Creativity occurs in a social context. Even when the creative product can be traced to the efforts of only one individual, the fact of the matter is that one can always find the effects of the cultural context. The cultural context is the matrix in which the creative individual developed, was educated and trained, and in a real sense was prepared for creative work. It provides sources and materials to be used for hypothesis formation and hypothesis testing. For the last phase of the process, communication, it provides, among other things, various channels through which creative ideas and products may be disseminated. Just as the cultural context effects the efforts of creative individuals, so it also effects the nature of the adoption process and the readiness with which different subgroups in the population might accept creative works.

Among the various sociocultural factors that critically effect the creative process, here are several that are probably the more salient ones:

1. *Zeitgeist.* Is the society at the time that a work is undertaken characterized by curiosity and a desire for understanding? Or, is the society characterized by conservative attitudes and attitudes emphasizing traditionalism?

2. *Status of the field.* Is the field in which the individual works characterized by growth and many new developments, or is it in a state of saturation and decline? It is often easier to develop novelty in a period when an area is in a state of growth. When it is saturated, even valiant efforts may not produce much, if anything.

3. *Philosophical orientation of the culture.* The philosophical orientation of the culture provides the individual with both a framework for how to look at the surrounding world and also some kind of weighting system for determining the relative significance of what is perceived. An individual's philosophical orientation will affect what is selected and how it is interpreted and utilized in his work.

4. *Available technology.* Creative developments will not only depend on available natural resources, but also on available technological develop-

ments. The telescope was obviously crucial for many discoveries and developments in astronomy, as was the microscope in biology.

5. *Socioeconomic factors.* To explore, to be curious, and to be creative depend on numerous factors, but certainly they depend on the opportunities available to the individual to engage in such activities. In some societies, these opportunities may be limited to specific groups of individuals, either because they were born to the proper status or because they had adequate financial resources.

6. *Educational experiences.* Similarly, the opportunity available to be educated in the traditions, theories, and techniques of different fields is an important ingredient to an individual's creativity. Education involves more than techniques (e.g., it involves discipline, values, etc.).

7. *Language.* Language will affect thought processes. Some cultures lack specific terms, and hence individuals in that culture are handicapped in dealing with related concepts. Available terminology is certainly no assurance of creativity, but at least one conceptual handicap has been overcome.

8. *Child-rearing practices.* Cultures vary in their child-rearing practices. The direction of creativity may well be affected by early developmental experiences. Effects are evident both in the kind and amount of creativity that is manifest.

THE ORGANIZATION OR COMPANY: A SYSTEM AND
ITS SUBSYSTEMS

Within the sociocultural context, there are companies and other organizations built and developed to fulfill society's needs through the recruitment, management, and development of human resources (Schein, 1978). These organizations and companies may be regarded as systems with their own subsystems. Like all other systems, each is charged with or has selected for itself both maintenance and growth functions. The relative distribution of organizational energy and resources to each of these categories varies with each organization and reflects the scope of activity it has cut out for itself, its goals, profit orientation, value system, etc.

Maintenance functions refer to those functions that keep the organization in existence and in equilibrium. At a simple, concrete level, it refers to the maintenance of the physical structure—heating and lighting the plant, etc. Growth functions are oriented to increasing information, and one way of doing this is through creative works. One cannot exist without the other, although at any one point in time and for any one organization, one may be more important or more salient than another. A creative organization is oriented primarily or largely to growth. It may be characterized in a variety of ways as indicated in Table 6.1.

TABLE 6.1
Selected Characteristics of the Creative Organization[a]

Idea men
Open channels of communication
Encourages contact with outside
Heterogeneous personnel policy
Includes marginal, unusual types
Assigns nonspecialists to problems
Allows eccentricity
Objective, fact-founded approach
Ideas evaluated on merit, not status of originator
Selects and promotes on merit only
Lack of financial, material commitment to products, policies
Invests in basic research; flexible, long-range planning
Experiments with new ideas rather than prejudging on "rational" grounds; everything gets a
    chance
More decentralized, diversified
Administrative slack; time and resources to absorb errors
Risk-taking ethos; tolerates and expects taking chances
Not run as tight ship
Allows freedom to choose and pursue problems
Freedom to discuss ideas
Organizationally autonomous
Original and different objectives; not trying to be another "X"
Security of routine; allows innovation
Has separate units or occasions for generating versus evaluating ideas; separates creative from
    productive functions

---

[a] From Steiner, 1965, pp. 16–17.

To fulfill its goals, the organization or system recruits personnel to fill established positions in the organizational hierarchy. For each level of the hierarchical relationship, the organization establishes certain expectations, or what the sociologists call *roles*. To cut across differences in hierarchical status, I (Stein, 1962, 1974b) suggested that the researcher in industry has to fulfill five such roles: scientist, professional, administrator, employee, and social (Stein, 1959a, b, c, d, e). In fulfilling the *scientist* role, the industrial researcher has as his audience other scientists with whom he can speak an esoteric language and share his information, data, and results. The researcher, however, is also a *professional*. By definition, a professional is a person who has a *client*. Thus, doctors and lawyers are professionals and not scientists because they serve clients. The client for the researcher in industry is first and foremost the company. It is the company that comes to him with problems. In another sense, the client of the researcher is the customer. This is true even though the researcher may never see the customer.

Sooner or later, the researcher has to assume a third role—*administrator*. This role has two aspects. One of them is the administration *of* research, which involves responsibility for ongoing research studies, supervision of subordinates and assistants, and other activities directly related to research. The second aspect of this role is administration *for* research. This subrole focuses on paperwork, meetings, budgets, etc.

In addition to all else, the researcher, like other persons in the company, has an *employee* role. Whatever else he might be, the researcher has certain obligations and privileges as a company employee. He has seniority, has to punch a time clock, pick vacation times, etc. The last role is a *social* role and it deals with how the individual behaves socially. Some organizations tolerate a wide range of behavior. Other organizations are very strict and involve themselves not only with the individual's comportment on the job, but also with his manner and style of dress, etc. Similarly, organizations vary in the extent and degree to which they get involved in the individual's social role off the job. They may suggest or prescribe the clubs one should belong to, the sports one should play, etc.

The very roles of the researcher may contain within them the germs of future intra- and interpersonal stress and conflicts (Stein, 1974b; Stein, Heinze, & Rogers, 1958). Stress can result from value conflicts, as when the desire to fulfill role requirements so that one can be creative comes into conflict with the desire to fulfill role requirements so that one can be successful. Management can help diminish this kind of stress by providing two ladders for rising within the organization—one on which the individual rises by taking on more and more administrative responsibility and the other on which the individual rises by making creative contributions. Indeed, there are other kinds of stress that might require other solutions.

GROUPS

Let us now work our way down from the macrolevel of the organization to a small unit within it—the group—and look at its effects on creativity. Much of what we will say will sample a variety of laboratory studies of groups, but we shall also consider data from real life situations.

Group Norms and Group Pressures. Groups can moderate individual judgments (Sherif, 1936). With no external structure to guide them as they respond to external stimuli, individuals in a group develop a group norm. Extreme responses are brought into line through a process of normalization (Muscovici & Faucheux, 1979).

Individuals in a group who are seen as holding up the group's decisions on important matters are subjected to group pressure to get them into line

(Schachter, 1951). These pressures can become so intense that people inhibit themselves and produce responses of inferior quality (Whyte, 1956). Alone, a bystander may help someone in an emergency; if others are around, a person is less likely to do so (Latané & Darley, 1970).

Group pressure may be so intense for some people that they will agree with a group's perceptions even when the judgments are palpably incorrect (Asch, 1956; Tuddenham & McBride, 1959). When problem solving is involved, a group may be carried away by the cumulative responses of its members (valence of solution, Hoffman, 1959) and even stay with a solution that is less adequate than one offered later.

To overcome some of the negative group effects, managers might well profit from the work on *brainstorming and creative problem solving* (Parnes, 1967a, 1967b). I have summarized the research in this area elsewhere (Stein, 1975), but for our purposes here, I would like to call attention to some potentially helpful suggestions. One may gain added benefits from the use of brainstorming with a group by: separating idea evaluation from idea generation and not merely deferring judgment; using a procedure called *sequencing* (Bouchard, 1972), in which each individual, in turn, has an opportunity to offer suggestions and is not free to respond at will (which makes it possible for some persons to dominate the situation); to add the use of personal analogy (Gordon, 1961); to preselect group members for interpersonal effectiveness (Bouchard, 1972); to use a group to share information about a problem, but have group members generate solutions working alone and then collect and evaluate these solutions in the group (Dunnette, 1964). All of these suggestions are designed to allow for the advantages of individual deviation and to limit some of the effects of group pressure to conformity.

Group Facilitation. Working in a group need not necessarily inhibit one's behavior. Studies of subjects whose behavior is paced by another, the so-called coaction studies, which go way back (Triplett, 1897), indicate that a person's behavior is facilitated and stimulated when paced. This is a wide-ranging effect, for it is manifest among animals as well as humans (Zajonc, 1965, 1969).

Facilitation also occurs when an individual has an audience (Allport, 1924; Henchy & Glass, 1968; Zajonc, 1965; Zajonc & Sales, 1966). But here one has to be careful to note whether one is involved in quantity and–or quality of response. Quality of response may be negatively effected in a group.

Probably the extreme in group releasing effects is the "risky shift" phenomenon (Wallach & Kogan, 1965), according to which it was suggested that individuals in groups are more likely to take greater risks than when working alone. More recent results (Myers & Lamm, 1976) indicate that the shift does not work in only one direction. Effects in groups are polarized.

Managers need, therefore, to be aware that their subordinates might well profit from the facilitating effects of group membership. At the same time, however, they need to be aware of steamroller tactics, in which a group may become overstimulated and oversell itself.

Communication Networks. When a group of people get together to solve a laboratory problem (Bavelas, 1948, 1950; Leavitt, 1951), it has been found that centralized communication networks (with all information having to go to a central spot before being disseminated to all who are involved) provide great efficiency than decentralized networks. The latter, however, are better for group morale. If one wants to collect information in one place, then centralized networks are again better. If one expects to do something with this information, then the pendulum again swings to decentralization (Shaw, 1964).

Communication networks differ among various individuals in research and development organizations. As in other organizations, some of the men are oriented internally—the "locals"—and others are "cosmopolites," to borrow phrases from sociologists (Rogers & Shoemaker, 1971). Our research indicates that more and less creative researchers in our industrial studies used opposite networks to gather the same data. To gather information on what was going on in the company, more creative subjects went inside the company and less creative subjects went outside. However, to gather information that might be helpful with problems one was working on at the time, the more creative men turned outside the organization and the less creative men turned inside.

Becoming aware of one's communication networks and the degree of their effectiveness can be invaluable to a person's creativity.

Group Composition. The number of people in a group and the diversity of member characteristics are critical to the group's behavior: "the fact that two or more individuals possess the same resource does not increase the total set of available resources but does increase the probability of that resource being used" (Shiflett, 1979). It is, therefore, important to investigate group characteristics to determine if, on relevant matters, the group is homogeneous or heterogeneous. The research evidence in this regard suggests the following: Individuals who are fairly similar to each other are better at getting simple, routine tasks done than people who are dissimilar to each other. Dissimilar people, however, are better if the group has to work on complex tasks requiring creativity (Hoffman, 1959; Hoffman & Maier,

1961). These investigators also report data limited to dyads among whom it has been found that dyads heterogeneous in attitudes, but homogeneous in abilities, were more creative than those dyads who were heterogeneous or homogeneous in both sets of psychological characteristics. Also, it should be noted that the more creative each individual in a dyad is, the higher the creativity of the two-person team.

Gordon (1961) supports the value of heterogeneous groups using his *synectics* technique for stimulating creativity. And, in the field of advertising, one hears of numerous anecdotal reports attesting to the value of heterogeneous groups for creative works.

GROUP AGING

Groups, like individuals, age. A group may, however, retain its youthful characteristics if it has frequent infusions of new people, regardless of their chronological age. Group age, therefore, depends on how long the group has been together. What are the effects of such aging?

Among bomber crews, younger groups give more correct solutions to problems than older groups. A low-status member of a younger group feels freer to disagree than does one in an older group (Torrance, 1957). Creativity does peak rather early in a group's history. Superiors see it peaking earlier (16 months or less) than do group members (2–5 years) (Shepard, 1956).

Pelz and Andrews (1966), studying groups in research and development organizations found:

1. Scientific contribution declined with group age.
2. Usefulness (not to be confused with creativity) to the organization peaked at 4 or 5 years of group age and then declined.
3. Older groups were more relaxed, less secretive, and more specialized than younger groups.
4. If older groups maintained their interaction with others and kept up intellectually, then they also retained their vitality.
5. It should be noted, however, that not all relationships are monotonic with age. Pelz and Andrews developed a measure they called *intellectual tension,* based on such factors as how dissimilar group members see each other, secretiveness, etc., and they found that while it was a handicap to younger groups, it was a stimulant to older groups.

The data suggest, therefore, that managers keep group age in mind as they make up their groups, focusing on relationships that will maintain group vitality.

Management: An Intermediary in the Creative Process

We conceptualize management's function in the creative process as that of an intermediary—a function it shares with curators of museums, art gallery owners, foundation executives, etc., all of whom serve as "gatekeepers" (Lewin, 1958) for the society. They assess society's needs and select a number of them to be fulfilled by their organization. Within its industry, management can be a leader setting a pace for other companies or it may adopt a more defensive posture, spending its time and money keeping up with competitors who have already taken the lead. Whether leader or follower, management then seeks to invest its capital prudently, taking appropriate risks so that progress is insured and a profit is returned to investors.

Within the organization, managers fulfill the same roles—scientist, professional, administrative, employee, and social—as others do, except that they distribute their time and effort differently. The manner in which these roles are fulfilled effects subordinates' and colleagues' efforts, and hence the extent to which the organization's products do or do not come to fruition. Thus, the character of the manager's function as an intermediary is complete—to that of selector of society's needs, we have now added gatekeeper, selecting and–or rejecting that which will pass from within the organization into the society.

A manager's stress stems not only from role conflicts, but also from the fact that there is little structure that comes with the roles and functions that must be fulfilled. A subordinate has work "cut out for him or her;" a manager imposes his or her own structure. The role demands blend. One minute one may have to be administrator-for-research; the next a scientist–professional; soon thereafter one is in the social role. One can put one's own stamp on work, setting the tone for the office and establishing a hierarchy among the things one wants others to do. But more often than not, "there are so many fires to put out" that one is swamped. If one does not have a superb secretary for "protection," one can be lost. If one does not select subordinates properly, one can be overwhelmed.

THE MANAGERIAL PERSONALITY

To fulfill the job properly, to be ready to make decisions, to make proper decisions, demands of the manager not only appropriate cognitive characteristics, but also some pattern of personality characteristics. While all of the objective data are not yet in, and while there may be different patterns of personality characteristics that fulfill the same job, there is one that we have

TABLE 6.2
Stein Self-Description Questionnaire: Ideal
Types for Researchers and Administrators

Resourceful Type	Forceful Type
(Creative researchers)	(Administrators)
1. Achievement	1. Achievement
2. Affiliation	2. Counteraction
3. Counteraction	3. Aggression
4. Play	4. Autonomy
5. Order	5. Dominance
6. Dominance	6. Rejection
7. Sex	7. Defendance
8. Sentience	8. Sex
9. Exhibition	9. Affiliation
10. Nurturance	10. Order
11. Autonomy	11. Exhibition
12. Deference	12. Play
13. Harmavoidance	13. Sentience
14. Blamavoidance	14. Harmavoidance
15. Defendance	15. Infavoidance
16. Succorance	16. Blamavoidance
17. Infavoidance	17. Deference
18. Aggression	18. Nurturance
19. Rejection	19. Succorance
20. Abasement	20. Abasement

recently discerned that we call the *Forceful Type,* which we think is especially well matched to cope with situational demands.[4]

A ranking of needs obtained from the *Forceful Type* (Table 6.2), especially
those that are ranked at the top as well as those that are ranked at the bottom,
may be interpreted as indicating that this sort of person is oriented to working
hard to achieve important goals and to re-strive after encountering difficulty

[4] Top level managers in research and development were not available to us for this study.
Access to such managers was available only in other kinds of organizations. We don't know that
the two groups would be very different from each other. Nevertheless, the material presented is
only for illustrative purposes. The data were collected by means of the Stein Self-Description
Questionnaire (Stein, 1965, 1966; Stein & Neulinger, 1968) which requests the manager to rank
order 20 paragraphs, each of which describes a psychological need (Murray *et al.,* 1938). These
data are then analyzed to determine how close they come to already researched types, of which
there are a total of nine, including those discussed. Empirical data suggest that the *Forceful Type*
is found among top level managers, and the *Resourceful Type* is found more frequently among
creative researchers.

and even failure. He or she is an aggressive person who speaks out as necessary. He or she is independent, follows his or her own inclinations, and feels he or she is master of his or her destiny. This, in very brief form, is what one might say of such a person from the fact that achievement, counteraction, aggression, autonomy, and dominance are the first five ranked needs.

From the five needs that are at the bottom of the list we infer that this *Forceful Type* person is not inclined to avoid blame for his or her actions, is not inclined to defer to authority, does not care to take care of others or, for that matter, to be cared for or led by others, and lastly, this type of person does not feel subject to fate.

A manager with this type of personality–need constellation is quite capable of fulfilling the roles spelled out previously. He or she is certainly forceful enough to set the priorities necessary for the fulfillment of various roles. He or she is sufficiently autonomous and nondeferent to authority so that he or she can assert him or herself properly and seek the fulfillment of his or her goals. This person is not afraid of blame, is likely to be quite confident in his or her own judgment, and is not afraid of criticism for the compromises he or she feels have to be made.

While the personality pattern may predispose the manager to deal effectively with many job demands, it may clash with the personality pattern found in some subordinates, especially those who may be of the *Resourceful Type,* a type containing many creative persons. The order of needs for this type are also presented in Table 6.2, along with those of the *Forceful Type,* for ready comparison. Suffice it, for illustrative purposes, to point out a few of the differences between the two patterns.

Need achievement is ranked first in both the *Forceful* and *Resourceful Types,* indicating that both see themselves as ambitious and aspiring persons who accomplish difficult things. From there on in, the similarity ends. *Need Affiliation,* the desire to be with and get along with people, is ranked second by the *Resourceful Type,* but the same need is ranked ninth by the *Forceful Type.* However, *Need Aggression,* the need to overcome opposition forcefully, to fight and attack, to be argumentative and severe with others, is ranked third by the *Forceful Type* and eighteenth by the *Resourceful Type.* While *Forceful Type* managers may express their aggression, members of the *Resourceful Type* are more likely to repress or supress theirs.

To maximize the probability of arriving at good decisions, managers need not only be aware of their own personality dynamics, but also the personalities of others, so that managers can bring out the best in them for their contribution to the decision-making process. To allow personal needs to override the situation and to clash with others is to invite irrational and faulty decisions, but where they are utilized to further one's insights and to bring out the best in others, the possibility of arriving at a creative decision is increased.

Recommendations

My purpose in this chapter has been to elucidate the major requirements of the creative process; some of the psychological characteristics of those who are capable of fulfilling these characteristics; and the effects that organizations, groups, and managers (might) have on the creative process and the creative individual—all oriented to produce more creative decision makers and more effective decision-making processes. In conclusion, and with an emphasis on brevity, I limit myself to five recommendations, based on ideas presented previously. All of these are based on the assumption that creative decision making is a function of the transactional relationship between the individual and the environment (organization, group, interaction with manager) in which he or she is found. Creativity is a most valuable resource; those who are capable of it and those who effect it are valuable resources, too. Hopefully, the recommendations that follow will be of further help.

1. Managers would do well to acquaint themselves not only with the decision-making process, but also with the nature of the creative process and the psychological characteristics of individuals who are able to fulfill these processes. Managers are quite knowledgeable about the inventory and depreciation of their plant and major equipment, but they are often sorely lacking in appreciation of the dynamics of the creative process, the role they play in it, and their inventory of creative people.[5]

2. Managers should be more aware of their human resources and human capital. Pragmatically, they might well adopt accounting principles that regard their creative personnel not as involving labor costs, which are to be depreciated over time, but as assets, which are to be appreciated. If this orientation cannot be implemented concretely and in actuality, then it should play a role in the development of a new set of attitudes that emphasize the importance of creative persons to a company's and society's growth.[6]

[5] For example, it is not uncommon to hear a number of creative individuals complain of depressive periods. Obviously, the creative person is quite upset by this, for he or she feels "over the hill," and the manger is frequently upset that he or she now has to put the formerly creative individual "out to pasture." However, while there may be many reasons for the depression, it is not uncommon that a depression may be a precursor of creative things to come. Knowing the characteristics of one's "inventory," there would, obviously, not be a need to discard the "depressed" creative person, but rather to be reassuring and to sweat it out.

[6] In a recent international study, entitled *Scientific Productivity*, edited by Andrews (1979), we find the following statement early in the book devoted to an overview of the work. "With regard to the need for maximizing the output from national investment in R & D, it is certainly rewarding to the humanist that one of the major conclusions that emerges from the study points to the primary importance, for the performance effectiveness of research units, of the compe-

3. Human capital and resources should be surveyed and assessed at periodic intervals. Morale surveys in industry are already of proven value, but surveys designed specifically for personnel engaged in creative pursuits (and the technique of role analysis presented in this chapter is only one such) should be concentrated on. Such data, if utilized properly, can be of great value both to management and to the personnel managed. Comparisons of data obtained periodically would be of great value in determining where alterations or changes have to occur, as well as where the strengths and weaknesses are.

4. There is a sufficient body of knowledge available that should enable management to increase their number of "hits" in the selection process. There are prejudices against the use of tests, and indeed there are regulations that restrict their use. There is still much that can be done in the face of the latter, and the former needs to be overcome or at least tested in the face of objective data. Management need not be reactive, waiting for challenges here and abroad to increase their understanding of creative persons and the creative process. Permanent assessments for creativity should be instituted as part of company programs, along with their other assessment programs.

5. There are numerous procedures for stimulating the creativity of individuals and groups. Many of these can be quite useful and helpful. Some managers, however, are inclined to use these procedures in a random fashion. Their proper use involves selection based on organizational needs.

If use is made of these five recommendations, management will go a long way in utilizing the creative potential of personnel already in its employ and in fostering the creativity of those who are yet to come so that the organization profits from truly creative decision-making processes.

References

Allport, F. H. *Social psychology.* Boston: Houghton Mifflin, 1924.
Andrews, F. M. (Ed.), *Scientific productivity: The effectiveness of research groups in six countries.* New York: Cambridge University Press, 1979.
Asch, S. Studies in independence and conformity: A minority of one against a unanimous majority. *Psychological Monographs,* 1956, *70* (9, Whole No. 416).
Barron, F. The needs for order and disorder in creative activity. *In* C. W. Taylor (Ed.), *The 1957 research conference on the identification of creative scientific talent.* Salt Lake City: University of Utah Press, 1958.

---

tence and personality of the unit head, *together* with the satisfaction of the unit members vis-à-vis the quality and sufficiency of its human resources. Financial resources are not to be reckoned as number one in the national investments in R & D [pp. 12–13, italics in the quotation]."

Bavelas, A. A mathematical model for group structures. *Applied Anthropology,* 1948, 7, 16–30.

Bavelas, A. Communication patterns in task-oriented groups. *Journal of the Acoustical Society of America,* 1950, 22, 725–730.

Bennett, L. Organizing to overcome the pain of being different. *New York Times,* April 13, 1980.

Blatt, S. J. Patterns of cardiac arousal during complex mental activity. *Journal of Abnormal and Social Psychology,* 1961, 63, 272–282.

Blatt, S. J., & Stein, M. I. Efficiency in problem solving. *Journal of Psychology,* 1959, 48, 193–213.

Bouchard, T. J., Jr. A comparison of two group brainstorming procedures. *Journal of Applied Psychology,* 1972, 56, 418–421.

Bronson, G. Brakes on basics: Innovative research is taking back seat as chemical firms weigh costs, profits. *The Wall Street Journal,* June 2, 1976, 34.

Brown, R. A., & Luckcock, R. G. Dreams, daydreams and discovery. *Journal of Chemical Education,* 1978, 55, 694–696.

Dunnette, M. D. Are meetings any good for solving problems? *Personnel Administration,* March–April 1964, 29, 12–16.

Galton, F. *Hereditary genius.* New York: Appleton, 1870.

Gordon, W. J. J. *Synectics.* New York: Harper, 1961.

Hartmann, H. *Essays on ego psychology.* New York: International Universities Press, 1964.

Henchy, T., & Glass, D. C. Evaluation apprehension and the social facilitation of dominant and subordinate responses. *Journal of Personality and Social Psychology,* 1968, 10, 446–454.

Hoffman, L. R. Homogeneity of member personality and its effect on group problem solving. *Journal of Abnormal and Social Psychology,* 1959, 58, 27–32.

Hoffman, L. R., & Maier, N. R. F. Quality and acceptance of problem solutions by members of homogeneous and heterogeneous groups. *Journal of Abnormal and Social Psychology,* 1961, 62, 401–407.

Hofstadter, D. R. *Gödel, Escher, Bach: An eternal golden braid.* New York: Basic Books, 1979.

John, E. R. Contributions to the study of the problem-solving process. *Psychological Monographs,* 1957, 71 (18, Whole No. 447).

Joint Economic Committee of Congress, *Midyear review of the economy,* 1976.

Kris, E. *Psychoanalytic explorations in art.* New York: International Universities Press, 1952.

Kuhn, T. S. *The structure of scientific revolutions* (2nd ed. enl.). Chicago: University of Chicago Press, 1970.

Lasch, C. *The culture of narcissism.* New York: Norton, 1979.

Latané, B., & Darley, J. M. *The unresponsive bystander: Why doesn't he help?* New York: Appleton-Century-Crofts, 1970.

Leavitt, H. J. Some effects of certain communication patterns on group performance. *Journal of Abnormal and Social Psychology,* 1951, 46, 38–50.

Lederberg, J. Personal communication, 1980.

Lewin, K. Group decision and social change. In E. E. Maccoby, T. M. Newcomb, & E. L. Hartley (Eds.), *Readings in social psychology* (3rd ed.). New York: Holt, 1958.

MacKinnon, D. W. *The identification and development of creative potential.* Paper presented at Bowdoin College, Brunswick, Maine, May 2, 1964.

Murray, H. A. et al. *Explorations in personality.* New York: Oxford University Press, 1938.

Muscovici, S., & Faucheux, C. Social influence, conformity bias and the study of active minorities. In L. Berkowitz (Ed.), *Advances in experimental social psychology.* New York: Academic Press, 1979.

Myers, D. G., & Lamm, H. The group polarization phenomenon. *Psychological Bulletin,* 1976, 83, 602–627.

Nisbett, R. *History of the idea of progress.* New York: Basic Books, 1980.

Parnes, S. J. *Creative behavior guidebook.* New York: Scribner, 1967. (a)

Parnes, S. J. *Creative behavior workbook.* New York: Scribner, 1967. (b)

Pelz, D. C., & Andrews, F. M. *Scientists in organizations.* New York: Wiley, 1966.

Reichenbach, H. *Experience and prediction.* Chicago: University of Chicago Press, 1938.

Rogers, E. M., & Shoemaker, F. F. *Communication of innovations* (2nd ed.). New York: The Free Press, 1971.

Schachter, S. Deviation, rejection and communication. *Journal of Abnormal and Social Psychology,* 1951, *46,* 190–207.

Schein, E. H. *Career dynamics: Matching individual and organizational needs.* Massachusetts: Addison-Wesley, 1978.

Shaw, M. F. Communication networks. *In* L. Berkowitz (Ed.), *Advances in experimental social psychology.* New York: Academic Press, 1964.

Shepard, H. A. Creativity in R/D teams. *Research and Engineering,* October 1956, 10–13.

Sherif, M. *The psychology of social norms.* New York: Harper, 1936.

Shiflett, S. Toward a general model of small group productivity. *Psychological Bulletin,* 1979, *86,* 67–79.

Stein, M. I. *Individual qualification form.* New York: Abacus, 1959. (a)

Stein, M. I. *Personal data for scientific, engineering, and technical personnel.* New York: Abacus, 1959. (b)

Stein, M. I. *Research personnel review form.* New York: Abacus, 1959. (c)

Stein, M. I. *Stein research environment survey.* New York: Abacus, 1959. (d)

Stein, M. I. *Stein survey for administrators.* New York: Abacus, 1959. (e)

Stein, M. I. Creativity and the scientist. *In* B. Barber, & W. Hirsch (Eds.), *The sociology of science.* New York: The Free Press, 1962.

Stein, M. I. Creativity in a free society. *Educational Horizons,* 1963, *41,* 115–130.

Stein, M. I. Explorations in typology. *In* C. S. Hall, & G. Lindzey (Eds.), *Theories of personality.* New York: Wiley, 1965.

Stein, M. I. *Volunteers for peace.* New York: Wiley, 1966.

Stein, M. I. Creativity and culture. *In* R. L. Mooney, & T. A. Razik (Eds.), *Explorations in creativity.* New York: Harper, 1967.

Stein, M. I. Creativity. *In* E. F. Borgatta, & W. W. Lambert (Eds.), *Handbook of personality theory and research.* Chicago: Rand McNally, 1968.

Stein, M. I. *Physiognomic cue test.* New York: Behavioral Publications, 1974a.

Stein, M. I. *Stimulating creativity: Individual procedures* (Vol. 1). New York: Academic Press, 1974b.

Stein, M. I. *Stimulating creativity: Group procedures* (Vol. 2). New York: Academic Press, 1975.

Stein, M. I., & Neulinger, J. A typology of self-descriptions. *In* M. M. Katz, J. O. Cole, & W. E. Barton (Eds.), *The role and methodology of classification in psychiatry and psychopathology.* U.S. Public Health Service Publication No. 1584. Washington, D.C.: Government Printing Office, 1968.

Stein, M. I., Heinze, S. J., & Rodgers, R. R. Creativity and/or success. *In* C. W. Taylor (Ed.), *The Second (1957) University of Utah research conference on the identification of creative scientific talent.* Salt Lake City: University of Utah Press, 1958.

Steiner, G. (Ed.). *The creative organization.* Chicago: University of Chicago Press, 1965.

Torrance, E. P. *Guiding creative talent.* Englewood Cliffs, New Jersey: Prentice-Hall, 1962.

Torrance, E. P. et al. *Role of evaluation in creative thinking* (U.S. Office of Education, Department of Health, Education, and Welfare, Cooperative Research Project No. 725). Minneapolis: Bureau of Educational Research, University of Minnesota, 1964. Revised summary report.

Torrance, E. P., Rush, C. H., Kohn, H. B., & Doughty, J. M. *Fighter–interceptor pilot combat effectiveness: A summary report.* Lackland Air Force Base, Texas: Air Force Personnel and Training Research Center, November 1957.

Tripplett, N. The dynamogenic factors in pacemaking and competition. *American Journal of Psychology,* 1897, *9,* 503–533.

Tuddenham, R. D., & McBride, P. D. The yielding experiment from the subjects' point of view. *Journal of Personality,* 1959, *27,* 259–271.

von Bertalanffy, L. *General system theory.* New York: George Braziller, 1968.

Wallach, M. A., & Kogan, N. *Modes of thinking in young children.* New York: Holt, 1965.

Wallas, G. *The art of thought.* New York: Harcourt, 1926.

Werner, H. *Comparative psychology of mental development.* New York: International Universities Press, 1957.

Wertheimer, M. *Productive thinking.* New York: Harper, 1945.

Whiting, C. S. *Creative thinking.* New York: Reinhold, 1958.

Whyte, W. H., Jr. *The organization man.* New York: Simon and Schuster, 1956.

Will the slowdown in new-product introductions continue? *The Wall Street Journal,* February 21, 1980, p. 1.

Zajonc, R. B. Social facilitation. *Science,* 1965, *149,* 269–274.

Zajonc, R. B. (Ed.), *Animal social behavior.* New York: Wiley, 1969.

Zajonc, R. B., & Sales, S. M. Social facilitation of dominant and subordinate responses. *Journal of Experimental Social Psychology,* 1966, *2,* 160–168.

Index